# TALES OF OLD INNS

*The yard of the* Beaufort Arms, *Monmouth.*
*The architecture of the yard is Georgian.*
(See Chapter 9)

# Tales of Old Inns

\*

*Richard Keverne*

\*

Revised and edited by Hammond Innes
With 74 illustrations
10 pen and ink drawings and 6 maps

COLLINS
14 ST JAMES'S PLACE LONDON
Published in association with Trust Houses Limited

THIS BOOK IS SET IN FONTANA, A TYPE FACE
DESIGNED FOR THE EXCLUSIVE USE OF THE
HOUSE OF COLLINS, AND PRINTED BY THEM
IN GREAT BRITAIN


FIRST PUBLISHED | MAY, 1939
SECOND IMPRESSION | DECEMBER, 1939
SECOND EDITION, REVISED AND RESET | MAY, 1947
THIRD EDITION | MAY, 1949
FOURTH EDITION | JANUARY, 1951
FIFTH EDITION | OCTOBER, 1952


COLLINS CLEAR-TYPE PRESS: LONDON AND GLASGOW

## DEDICATION

To those who love England's old country inns, I offer this book with every wish for good travelling, pleasant adventures, a warm welcome at the day's end, and, in some cosy coffee-room or snug bar, over a winter fire, or in some shady garden in the cool of a summer evening, a sympathetic stranger to talk to. And at the journey's end, new tales of old inns to tell.

RICHARD KEVERNE

# CONTENTS

# ILLUSTRATIONS

9

# ILLUSTRATIONS

# ILLUSTRATIONS

# PEN AND INK DRAWINGS

*Drawings by H. N. Eastaugh with exception of the detail on page 105 which is by Francis W. Reader.*

## MAPS

*Maps drawn by Dorothy Mahoney.*

# FOREWORD

The old Saxon word "Inn" has a warm welcoming ring. It is a traveller's word. The dictionary defines it as "a house for the lodging and entertainment of travellers." Hotel, tavern, public-house, victualling house, road-house, coffee-house—these are all inns when the keepers of them make it their business to furnish the traveller with food and lodging. The English inn has a great tradition. Down through the centuries, its hospitality has been remarked by the foreign traveller in Britain. Its heyday was the Coaching Era and along the great coaching roads of Britain the old inns flourished and expanded to meet the demands of the ever-increasing road traffic.

The railways and Victorian snobbery came near to killing the inn. The traffic left the roads and the old coaching houses became but ghosts of their former selves. But the inn survived as the centre of small communities and, with the arrival of the motor coach and motor car, the inn began to flourish again. The people began to flock out in their thousands on what had once been the coaching roads in an effort to escape from the drabness of city life. And, in the period between the wars, the inns of England became even more prosperous than in the Coaching Era. During the war, they played their part and there were few soldiers overseas who, when they thought of home, did not also remember some snug bar or quaint little roadside inn with affection. Now, once again, traffic has returned to the roads—good metalled roads now, but roads that follow the line of the old coach roads. And on these roads, many famous inns are there to welcome those who had little opportunity to travel the high-roads of Britain during the war.

This book was written to introduce the traveller to these famous old inns of ours. It is the personal story of the old country inns of Britain. It takes you along the old coaching roads and into the yards of famous hostelries that once rang with the stamp of horses' hooves and the shouts of ostlers and post-boys. It tells their story

15

and how they grew from tavern or ale-house to the great inns of to-day. It tells something of their history and much of what to look for in the actual building, so that the mind can form a picture of what the inn was like in the old days. It gets you acquainted with these old inns, so that you can enter them, not as a stranger, but as a friend, knowing them as you know your own home. It is a reminder, too, that through the centuries travellers have been stopping at these fine old inns, bringing to them a little of the atmosphere of each period in our history.

To some, this book will be an old friend, for it was first published in 1939. New editions have been issued because the publishers felt that, with so many people looking forward to re-visiting old haunts or discovering new ones, it was a pity that such an interesting introduction to the inn should remain out of print. Revision was necessary, for war hit the inns of Britain with little regard for their beauty or antiquity. Several inns mentioned in the original book have disappeared. These have been replaced by others in this new edition, so that the book is in no way less representative of our old inns than the original.

Unfortunately, the author, Richard Keverne, who died in 1949, was ill and could not undertake this revision. When I was asked to revise and edit the new edition of his book, I was glad to do so, because I had been out of Britain for a long time and had many pleasant memories of these old inns. I now have many more and I hope this book will make as many friends for you among the old inns of Britain as it has for me.

Richard Keverne collected the material for this book over a period of nearly twenty years. He travelled the old coach roads, talked to landlords and "oldest inhabitants," read through old newspaper files and books on old inns, searched old records with the help of librarians and hunted through museums with the assistance of the curators. He had a quick eye for detail and in this very extensive tour, covering more than 100 inns, both large and small in England and Wales, little escaped him by way of story, atmosphere or point of architectural interest. His book does all but strip the plaster from the walls to show you how these old inns were built and why and where to look for the little curiosities

*At the* White Hart, *Chipping Norton.  A once open gallery, enclosed in later years as a protection against the weather.*
(See Chapter 1)

*A " Coaching" or " Act of Parliament" clock on the wall by the*
*old staircase of the* George *at Cranbrook.*
(See Chapter I)

peculiar to very ancient inns. But it is always with the inn as it stands now that it deals, so that you can see for yourself and reconstruct the past from the present. And it tells many strange tales of interest to those who remember that these old inns have kept open house to every sort of traveller for centuries.

For convenience, the inns are grouped topographically and, wherever possible, they are described in tours easily followed by car, or, for the inn-lover without a car, by that modern stage-coach, the motor coach.

Richard Keverne had a great love for these old inns, and because of this and the patient years he spent in seeking out their story, his writing has a fond warmth that makes the old beams glow in the firelight and fills the inns with the busy noise of arrival and departure as you wander in his company through the old rooms, down into the cellars and out into the courtyard. His book brings to life all the bustle and excitement of the days when much of a town's interest was centred on the arrival of the "Diligence" or the "Telegraph" or the "True Blue" with its steaming horses and mud-caked wheels.

HAMMOND INNES.

# CHAPTER ONE

## *The Patchwork English Inn*

THE OLD INN is a patchwork thing: it had to be. A successful inn was one that moved with the times. It had to be constantly modernised, new accommodation added, old rooms brought up to date by alteration and redecoration. As public taste changed so the inn had to change, though carrying on its business all the while. For an inn, like a church, must never close its doors.

It is because of these patchings that the old inn has so much charm. In it you find bits and pieces of the craftsmanship often of four hundred years, sometimes, as at the *Angel* at Grantham, of six.

As they patched and altered, they were always aiming to improve their houses. The seventeenth-century landlord who put oak panelling over mid-sixteenth-century wall paintings at the *White Swan* at Stratford-on-Avon was no vandal. He simply counted his painted decorations shabby and old-fashioned. His customers preferred this new wainscoting that was all the fashion. So he gave it to them. Some three hundred years later a new proprietor removed the Jacobean panelling, by then grown rare, and found the even more rare decoration behind.

So with oak beams and ceilings. What pleased one generation displeased another. They covered them up, plastered the ceilings and papered the walls. And we should be grateful, for so much of the old work in this way has survived to be appreciated by a generation in love with ancient things.

The great rebuilding of inns that went on in the prosperous Posting Era was responsible for the destruction of a lot of old work. But that with which it was replaced has already become charming in our eyes. Only for the black, middle Victorian taste have we no sympathy. That was a naughty period, and yet maybe it will please the inn-lover of fifty years hence. At any rate, he will be able to read in it a chapter of the house's history which was written when

19

the English inn had fallen from favour, was counted by the genteel a mere public-house and used reluctantly in case of necessity only.

Properly to appreciate an old inn's tales you must look for these chapters written in stone and plaster, wood and wallpaper, odd fittings and conventional design. You will find the older survivals in the more neglected parts of the inn, the attics, the cellars, the top floor rooms, which were the cheaper ones and consequently had less attention given to them, and the abandoned buildings about the once bustling stableyards.

You may take it that most half-timbered inns of any consequence originally had open galleries on two or three sides of a courtyard. There is an example at the *George* at Huntingdon. The guest chambers led from these galleries which were approached by outside staircases. As time went on they closed in these galleries as a protection against the weather and in this condition a surprising number of them remain. There are references to some of the more obvious examples in the pages following. They are easily identifiable.

An inn-yard is a happy hunting ground for relics of the past. All sorts of "bygones" get stored away as lumber in its deserted buildings. The old loose-boxes nowadays are turned into garages, but the harness rooms and ostlers' rooms are generally to be found. And in some corner of the yard there is often a discarded mounting block used by our more portly forebears to help them into the saddle.

Above the stables in the bigger inns were the post-boys' quarters. The post-boy was a postilion who rode one of a pair of horses attached to a post-chaise. The traveller by chaise, a light carriage with a hood that could be opened, had perforce to change horses every few miles, generally ten to twelve or fifteen according to the condition of the road. This was a "stage." At each fresh stage a new pair and post-boy, or two pairs and two post-boys if the traveller were rich or in a hurry, were engaged. The first post-boy, when his horses were rested, would return with another chaise going to his inn. And since this posting trade was a very necessary and lucrative one, every posting inn had a large number of horses always ready, "at call" as the phrase was, hence the vast stables that still remain.

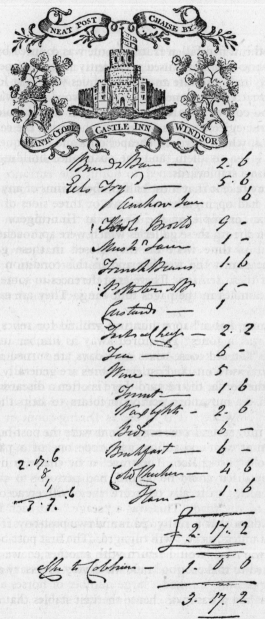

NEAT POST    CHAISE BY

WANTᴿ. CLODI    CASTLE INN    WINDSOR

| | |
|---|---|
| Wine & Bran | 2. 6 |
| Pete Fry | 5. 6 |
| | 6 |
| Anchovy Sauce | |
| Fresh Broild | 9 - |
| Mush.ᵒ Sauce | 1 - |
| French Beans | 1. 6 |
| Potatoes &c | 1 - |
| Custards | 1 |
| Tarts & cheese | 2. 2 |
| Tea | 6 - |
| Wine | 5 |
| Fruit | 1. 6 |
| Wax lights | 2. 6 |
| Beds | 6 - |
| Breakfast | 6 - |
| Cold Chicken | 4. 6 |
| Ham | 1. 6 |
| | £ 2. 17. 2 |
| Chaise to Cobham | 1. 0. 0 |
| | 3. 17. 2 |

2. 17. 6
8
1
3. 7. 6

*An inn bill of 1806.  Reproduced from the original.*

Behind the inn-yard, seek the garden and the bowling-green. Most old inns had big kitchen gardens and bowling-greens, and fortunately both these features have frequently been maintained. But the Brew Houses, another characteristic of the big inn-yard, have gone—out of use at any rate. You sometimes find them deserted and neglected, and see their copper utensils used for decoration in the public rooms of the inn.

The arch that leads to the yard has often a story to tell. Sometimes it has been heightened to admit the entrance of coaches. Often there are hooks left in its roof from which game and joints hung in a cooling breeze.

Look for the old kitchen just inside the archway, more often than not on the right. And in the kitchen look above the fireplaces for survivals of the racks that held the spits that pierced joints and birds in the days when they were roasted before an open fire, not baked in an oven. And look for relics of the roasting jacks that turned the spits. Sometimes you will find the jack complete though no longer in use.

The "Long Room" to which you will find many references in this book was a Georgian convention. It was known by many names: the "Great Room," the "Big Room," the "Assembly Room." It is nearly always on the first floor with a window leading on to the top of the porch, the room of big functions, dinners and dances. It usually had a movable partition or folding doors so that it could be divided. Nowadays it is in use as Dining-room or Lounge, or broken up into several bedrooms. It usually had a fireplace of the same design at each end and an ante-chamber leading from it. So where the old "Long Room" has been divided its former size may be traced by discovering the second fireplace, and if you examine the intervening walls the odds are they will prove to be mere partitions.

It was seldom that a really old inn was completely rebuilt in the Posting Era unless, as you will often read in these tales, it was burnt down. It was the front block to the street that was rebuilt or reconditioned to make a good modern show; so seek the older parts in the wings.

Old inns had a habit of changing their signs. As often as not the change was made by a new landlord who followed a bad one and sought to get rid of a sign that had acquired a bad name. Sometimes there was a political significance, sometimes it was purely arbitrary. The frequent change to the something "Arms" was an affectation of refinement that began in the later 1700's and became more common in the next three or four decades. No really old inn first hung out the sign of somebody's arms, any more than it called itself an "Hotel." It was content to be known bluntly as the *White Horse* or the *Star*, the *George* or *Red Lion Inn*, and put out a bold sign for the information of a generation of which few could read.

There is mention of Trade Tokens in some of these tales. They might be described as unofficial coins, halfpennies and farthings usually, issued by the leading traders in the middle 1600's. They were issued to provide small change of which there was a great lack at the time. Their issuers were men of standing who guaranteed to redeem their tokens in coin of the realm, and these tokens passed freely in circulation, not only in the towns of their issue, but for many miles around. The existence of an innkeeper's token is a very certain assurance that his inn at that time was of considerable importance.

As to the origin of the "Coaching Clock" so often found in an old Posting House, there is some uncertainty. It is known also as the "Inn Clock" and the "Act of Parliament Clock." The generally accepted explanation of the latter name is that this type of clock was introduced in 1797 when a tax was imposed upon private timepieces and many people gave up their own clocks. So the innkeeper provided a public clock for the convenience of his patrons. But the "Coaching Clock" was in use before 1797. Other tales tell vaguely of a law which compelled landlords of coaching inns to provide a standard clock for their houses. But the fact remains that they are of a distinctive type associated with inns. Their cases are nearly always plain, with a simple decoration on a black ground, and varnished. And we may take it that their reason for being was much the same as that of a clock in a railway station: that travellers might always know the correct time.

Of other characteristics of old inns perhaps the rarest is the chequered or lozenge sign of which possibly that at the *Methuen Arms* at Corsham is the only one left. It was the common sign of a tavern for centuries, and it probably has only survived at Corsham because it was painted on stone. On plaster or woodwork it would have been painted or whitewashed over years ago. So look for it in a stone country, on the door-posts of what was the chief bar entrance, not the main entrance to the inn. And if you ever happen on it, beg, bribe or threaten the landlord into preserving it.

You will find, as you study old inns, that they run very true to type. Their plan is as conventional as that of a church. But the plan is confused by later accretions. In seeking it out use detective methods, following up clues from room to room, watching the run of the main chimney, frequently the oldest part of the house, the base of which you may discover in an unaccountable sort of buttress in the cellar. Follow old moulded beams and cornices to ceilings and they will tell you of big rooms divided. It is the same with old tales, and traditions. Age has distorted them, but there is generally an ancient truth behind the garbled modern version. Read the tradition of the Plymouth Brethren at the *Red Lion* at Luton to exemplify this.

Patiently studying each patch in the jumbled fabric or tale you will find it joining up with another presently to make something of a whole to form a readable chapter of the inn's story.

They are still patching old inns, marking them as definitely with a tale of the second half of the twentieth century for future amateurs to read, as the "Long Room" tells to-day of the last half of the eighteenth. They are closing up the archways to the yards to form entrance halls or lounges. The lover of old inns can but deplore it. But the inn must be practical. The archway was for the horse: that has gone. The motor car goes in by the back entrance to the yard to garage in an old loose-box. So often, as at the *Swan* at Lavenham, the archway divided the house, and when it was no longer essential to the business of the inn, it became just an inconvenience. And the inn only survives, it must be remembered, where the landlords have adapted their houses to meet the changing needs of their patrons. But in many cases, like the one quoted, the old

*Perhaps a unique survival of an ancient inn custom. The painted lozenge or chequered design on the door posts of the Bar at the* Methuen Arms *at Corsham. This was the customary sign of the tavern in past days.*

(See Chapter 1)

One of a series of middle-sixteenth century wall paintings of the story of Tobit at the White Swan, Stratford-on-Avon. This was hidden behind panelling for three hundred years.

(See Chapter 1)

*The* Ferry Boat *at Tottenham on the River Lea. A fishing inn within half an hour of Piccadilly Circus.*
(See Chapter 2)

*A House with a pictorial sign.* *The* Saracen's Head *at Dunmow.*

(See Chapter 2)

outline of the archway has been left, so that the general appearance of the inn has not been seriously altered.

That is the way an inn should be modernised. The architect must be a man who understands and has a feeling for old things, and so must the builder and his workmen. To pull down and build afresh is so often the quickest and easist thing to do, and so much less expensive. Because of this, a great many of our old inns have disappeared or been entirely bereft of their original character during this century. The policy of the owners of the inns varies. In some cases there is complete disregard for antiquity. The commercially-minded will often inform their builders that speed in the alterations is all they ask. Sometimes an attempt is made to conform in the renovations to the original structure, but the architect and builders have insufficient experience. In either case, the results are disastrous. But during the years before the war, there was a growing tendency to regard antiquity as an asset in a house, and, therefore, to preserve the old appearance even through drastic alterations. The public has passed through the stage in which everything had to be modern and chromium-plated and there has developed now a very widespread and genuine love for old things.

But the desire to maintain the old appearance of an inn must not be allowed to check its development. An inn is not a public monument, however old. And its charm is that it has reacted architecturally to the various periods of our history. If more travellers pass through a town, then the town's inns must expand. If travellers want lounges, and wash-basins in the bedrooms, then they must be provided, regardless of whether they fit in with the appearance of the inn as a "period piece." But in all these changes, whether expansion or alterations to make the inn more up to date, they should be made to conform to the old pattern of the inn and to preserve as much as possible of the original fabric of the house. This costs money and requires both patience and experience.

It is interesting what a wealth of fine, old work can be uncovered during renovations to these old inns. At Lavenham, for instance, the lovely, half-timbered front was concealed behind a flat façade, the gables of which were edged with plaster frills so that there was little indication from the outside of the place as it is to-day. The

*Bull* at Long Melford was another; at one time the inn presented to the street a flat brick front with a stone coping. Behind was the old half-timbered face and the mellow tile roof that you see to-day. In renovations here, the half-timbering was exposed, but on the ground floor it was in such a bad state that it was not possible to retain the old structure. A new wall was, therefore, built after the style of the old, so that the inn retains its original appearance.

We must remember, whilst looking at these old inns, that they are commercial undertakings. They are adjusting themselves to the ever-changing needs of the times and they will go on adjusting themselves. If the public want old inns, then the old inns will be preserved. But if the public taste changes violently, then those old half-timbered houses will gradually disappear. That is the fascination of these old inns. They are essentially a patchwork, architecturally sympathetic to the public taste of each age they serve. That is how they survive and how they will continue to survive. And that is why they are perhaps the most characteristically English of all our institutions.

# CHAPTER TWO

## *Into East Anglia: Essex*

BECAUSE BUILDING stone is hard to come by in the Eastern Counties they are never so ready to pull down the old houses there as they were in other parts of the country. And so, strewn along the East Anglian roads, there are a satisfying number of those grand, half-timber inns that honest craftsmen put up three, four and sometimes nearly five hundred years ago.

They worked well, those old craftsmen, adorning their great oak timbers with skilful and curious carvings and decorating the plaster of the panels in between with moulded designs. And although in the Coaching Era innkeepers sometimes, to modernise their houses, erected ugly, flat, brick fronts that hid the early black and white work, they did little permanent harm.

There are two great roads out from London to the east, the one through Epping Forest, the other, and more important one, by Romford and Chelmsford. They meet at Norwich, and throw out many big tributaries on the way. But start your journey through Epping Forest and stop at an old riverside inn before you are clear of London.

This is on no old coach road, but on the route the modern motor cars take, out by the Seven Sisters' Road, through Tottenham to Woodford. The *Ferry Boat* it is called and it stands just into Essex across the bridge over the river Lea, beyond Tottenham.

It was the Ferry inn before they first bridged the river in 1760, and the periodical Courts of two neighbouring Manors were held there. But with the bridge came through traffic and greater prosperity to the road, and somewhere about 1760 the old *Ferry Boat* inn rebuilt itself. It has been enlarged and altered since but a good deal of the original work has survived. Two of the upstair rooms are wainscoted and there are remains of panelling on the landings. A hundred-odd-year-old oil painting of the house

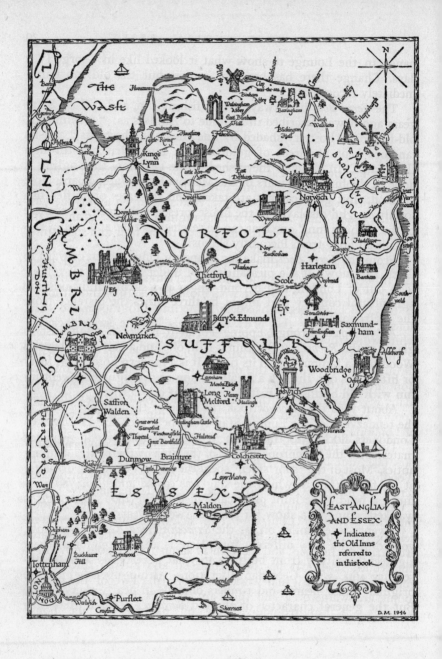

hangs in the Lounge to show what it looked like in George IV.'s days. Change there has been, of course, but the old inn is immediately recognisable.

The *Ferry Boat* has always been a fishing inn, and still is. Sixty years ago it was described in a Guide to Anglers as: "A rambling, old-fashioned hostelry shaded by fine elms and chestnuts," and its landlord kept hundreds of goldfish in a moat that ran through the garden. In old days they fished in the Lea, now the angling is done in the huge reservoirs of the Metropolitan Water Board, close at hand. But good catches are taken, and the cases of stuffed fish locally caught, displayed in the house, preserve the true atmosphere of the "fishing inn," one that can be reached by tube and trolley-bus in half an hour from Piccadilly Circus!

From the *Ferry Boat* make for Chipping Ongar, then onward to Great Dunmow. It is a pleasant run of under forty miles; you are soon out of London, and beyond Ongar is a surprisingly unspoilt agricultural country that might be three times the distance from the Metropolis.

As you pass through Epping Forest it is worth while just to glance at the *Roebuck* at Buckhurst Hill, one and a half miles beyond Woodford, a famous inn in its time. It is a modern hotel now, forty or fifty years old, though a small portion of the eighteenth-century inn with old beams and rafters survives at one corner.

About 1850 the *Roebuck* took the place of the *Baldfaced Stag* as the rendezvous of the Epping Stag Hunt held each Easter Monday. Londoners flocked to this hunt in their thousands and provided material for the humorous writers of the time by their extraordinary antics. Most of the "sportsmen" spent the day in eating and drinking at the forest inns to which the stag was carted and displayed at so much a head. The hunt practically died in the 1860's although it was kept going as a show for another twenty years.

Twenty-seven miles on, at the *Saracen's Head*, Great Dunmow, you come to a very different inn. Here is an example of a severe eighteenth-century front built on to what is certainly a sixteenth-century inn, with Georgian alterations within upon which the original Tudor beams and timbers obtrude in nearly every room. But the general character of the old *Saracen's Head* is that of a prosperous posting-house, though its tales go back a deal further than the posting days.

It was always an inn of importance and had for a landlord in the early 1600's the father of Sir Richard Deane, Lord Mayor of London in 1629. The Deanes were ardent Parliamentarians during the Civil War, and Oliver Cromwell sometimes stayed at the *Saracen's Head*.

Another old-time landlord, less worthy but more romantic, is one whose fame is remembered in Great Dunmow, though his name is forgotten. He was counted a worthy, pious man and a sympathetic and careful host, always solicitous of the welfare of his guests. They would confide in him their fears and their plans and he would advise them how to avoid the dangers of the road. He flourished amazingly until he had the misfortune to be caught robbing one of his own guests on the King's Highway. Then it was discovered that the fellow habitually combined the calling of highwayman with that of innkeeper, and was hand in glove with the smugglers of the coast too. Many a cargo of uncustomed liquor, run up an Essex creek of a moonless night, found its way furtively into the *Saracen's Head's* cellars in his time.

Many reminders of the inn's coaching and posting past have survived in the mounting block, ostlers' bell, stables and harness room in the yard. The Smoking-room was the Farmers' Room, where they gathered in other days. The bar is a most inviting place, one of those spacious, yet cosy rooms with low, beamed ceiling that seems not to have changed for a hundred years past. There is some old panelling left there into which an eighteenth-century clock by John Fordham, a Dunmow maker, is set. And the same simple gossip goes on night after night as it has done for generations past. There is much good Georgian furniture in the house; mahogany tables, tallboys and sideboards all suggesting tales of the inn's importance in the days when they were new.

Opposite the inn, in the half-timbered Town Hall, the famous "Flitch of Bacon" ceremony was revived for a while in the middle of the last century. This ceremony rightly belongs to the adjoining parish of Little Dunmow just over two miles away, where by ancient custom : "He which repents him not of his marriage, either sleeping or waking, in a year and a day," as the old record put it, might lawfully go and fetch a "Gammon of Bacon." The Gammon became a flitch in later years. Chaucer made reference to this old custom of the Manor, and the chair in which the claimants sat is still to be seen in Little Dunmow's Priory church.

Little Dunmow is on your direct way to the *White Hart* at Braintree, nine miles off; but it is worth while to go first to Saffron Walden and work your way back to Braintree by another road. It means a detour of about thirty miles, but one through delightful country. Happily the world does not yet know how remote and unspoiled is this simple, undulating land of North Essex.

The road, an old one, the cross-road from Rochford to Cambridge of coaching days, takes you in six miles from the *Saracen's Head* to Thaxted, an old wool town, with a lovely church, a Moot Hall built in James I.'s reign and a number of delightful half-timbered houses, and in another seven and a half to the *Rose and Crown* in Saffron Walden's Market Place. And there you run up against William Shakespeare.

The Shakespeare association with the inn is controversial; but it has been suggested that the elusive "Mr. W. H." to whom Shakespeare dedicated the *Sonnets*, was William Holgate, son of a landlord of the *Rose and Crown*. Young Holgate, himself a poet, was contemporary with many of the greatest literary men of Shakespeare's time, and the claim was first made by an eminent book-lover and student, Mr. Edmund Dring, on the strength of a manuscript book of William Holgate's that came into his possession a few years ago.

Mr. Dring's theory though much debated is now not generally approved; but we know that Shakespeare visited the town with a company of play-actors in 1607 and there can be little doubt that he knew and stayed at the inn. It has other literary associations too. Thomas Nash, the famous Elizabethan satirist, attacked one Gabriel Harvey, who lived next door but one to the *Rose and Crown*, in his "Have with you to Saffron Walden?" and in the next century a local poet, William Winstanley, mentioned the inn in his "Perambulation from Saffron Walden to London" published in 1678. He writes:

"... I'll show you whence my journey I did trace,
      It was from the *Rose and Crown* where Mr. Eve
      Doth keep a house like to an under Sheriff.
      There is good sack, good French wine and good beer."

The name of Landlord Eve frequently crops up in the town's
records. It was he who entertained the Mayor's party in 1680, when
King Charles II. visited Audley End, a magnificent Jacobean mansion,
until recently the seat of Lord Braybrooke, two miles away. Of that
occasion, the Corporation accounts record: "Pd. Mr. Eve for wine
at the Dinner . . . when we delivered the Address . . . £5 2s. 0d."
Good wine cost about eight shillings a gallon in those days!

Many changes have taken place at the *Rose and Crown* since
young William Holgate and William Winstanley wrote their poems,
and Gabriel Harvey and Thomas Nash and probably Shakespeare
himself drank and talked over the inn's cosy fires. The date of an
important change is recorded, for in 1916 an inscription on parch-
ment was discovered under a bedroom floor, which read: "This
house was fronted with brick in the year 1690, by William Patch
owner and keeper of the same, and the same was new sashed and
beautified in the year 1748." William Patch's new brick front was
restored in 1874.

There is a lot of decoration of the later sixteen and earlier
seventeen hundreds left in the house, including stretches of panelling
and a very fine staircase that William Patch may have installed.
Moulded plaster decoration—parge work they call it—may be seen
on some of the outside walls, and there is a good deal of the earlier
Tudor construction left, parts of an inn that was twenty or thirty
years old when Shakespeare came to the town.

The *Rose and Crown* can be ranked high among the more
interesting of old English inns, and for one who seeks their stories
it is a most tantalising place, for you feel that not a tithe of its tales
has yet been told.

For those who cross the border into Cambridgeshire, the *Blue
Boar* at Cambridge is worth looking at. There has been an inn of this
name standing in Trinity Street since 1552, although the sign hung
outside a house on the opposite side of the street in those days, and

*The restored 1748 front of the* Rose & Crown *at Saffron Walden, an inn with a Shakespeare tradition.*

(See Chapter 2)

*The* Red Lion *at Colchester, a museum specimen of half-timbered construction built about 1470.*

(See Chapter 2)

*The old wing of the* Blue Boar, *Maldon, which contains fabric of the
fourteenth century. In the foreground is a mounting block.*

(See Chapter 2)

*Mr. Pickwick, Mr. Peter Magnus, Weller Senior and Sam arrive at the* Great White Horse, *Ipswich, from London. (From the original painting by J. Temple).*

(See Chapter 3)

was transferred to the present inn at a later date. The earliest record of the *Blue Boar* on its present site is an entry in the Parish records of All Saints' Church, dated 1693, which discloses a payment of two shillings "for Beer at ye blue boar on ye Queen's birthday."

It has a long reputation as a coaching and posting inn. In 1753 two coaches ran between the *Bull* and *Green Dragon* in Bishopsgate and the *Blue Boar*, and by 1796 the stream of travellers journeying between Cambridge and London necessitated six coaches. In 1839 eight coaches made the journey to Cambridge, and "Hobson's Stage," the "Bee Hive" and the "Union" all set down their passengers in the courtyard of the *Blue Boar*.

An interesting photograph of 1879, which hangs in this Entrance Lounge, gives a rough idea of the old yard and stable buildings. It shows a hansom cab in the yard and immediately above it the inn's old stone sign of a Boar set in a niche in the wall. In the Entrance Hall, the old yard pump is said to be still in existence, covered by an angular casing against the Smoking Room wall. The coachway in past times was from Trinity Street, by the present entrance, through what was the yard and out through the present garage into Green Street.

The only old room remaining is what was the Coffee Room. The Smoke Room, on the opposite side of the Entrance Lounge, occupies the site of the old kitchen. This conforms with a common feature of old inns, that of having the Coffee Room and the Kitchen on opposite sides of the yard.

The original cellars remain, and the old entrance for barrels is still in use. This is now in the Entrance Lounge—the old yard—and the cellar flaps are covered by the Lounge carpet. The rest of the house has been modernised beyond recognition, but, oddly enough, despite its modernisation, the *Blue Boar* retains an atmosphere of the old inn.

Those who spend the night in Cambridge may prefer to shorten the route and pick it up again through Newmarket at the *Bell* at Thetford, for we are doubling back on our tracks now from Saffron Walden to Braintree by a different, but equally attractive road, through Radwinter and Great Sampford. Stop just to look at the unusual church here, and as a good traveller by road remember with gratitude John McAdam who did so much to create the modern road, even though his name be only remembered now in the "mac" of the tarmac over which you travel. McAdam lived in Great Sampford. Then on through Finchingfield and presently in to Braintree and the *White Hart* at the intersection of two Roman roads.

That suggests a long pedigree for the inn, for men have been travelling along these roads for close on two thousand years and there are few more certain places in which to find an ancient inn than where two main roads cross. There is just a chance that beneath the *White Hart's* cellars Roman work remains. But that is romantic surmise. The inn itself can only show four-century-old work and much of that has recently been uncovered, for as was the custom they modernised the old place in the Coaching Era.

The oldest work is in the block facing the main street. There, in the bar, are moulded ceiling beams and wall timbers of early Tudor date. There is more fine old timber work exposed in the Lounge and in some of the rooms above. Two long, low wings once enclosed the courtyard, with open galleries from which the guest chambers led. A survival of that gallery, since walled in, appears immediately to the right of the archway looking from the yard. The old room bells still hang by the entrance, and within the archway itself are two points of interest. A little, now closed door to the left as you enter once led to the chamber of the inn's night porter, who was thus ever at hand to open the great oak doors to the late arriving chaise or the benighted traveller clattering into Braintree in the small hours of the morning. Above your head there is a long iron bar such as still may be seen in old-fashioned butcher shops. From this the inn's game and joints were suspended in warm weather that they might be kept fresh by the cool breeze that blew through. And there are gourmets to-day who vow that there is no better way of hanging game than in such conditions and that birds will hang longer, and eat with finer flavour, without getting "too high," if they are always exposed to a breeze.

The yard is a charming place of irregular, tiled roofs and whitewashed walls. There is some old timber work worth noting in the range of stables on one side, and although the ugly, two-storied grey building that occupies part of the other may seem incongruous, it contains some attractive decoration of the end of the Georgian period, a graceful curving staircase, and delicately designed fanlights above the doors. It was built just over a hundred years ago as a Ball and Assembly Room. "Large and Elegant" these rooms were described when they were new-built and, apart from Assemblies, Petty Sessions and the County Court were held here for years, and a "News and Reading Room" was opened. Now the Dining-room occupies the ground floor, and the one above has been divided into bedrooms.

The way through the yard leads past a cosy, old-fashioned "Tap" to Braintree's Egg and Poultry Market, to which neighbouring farmers have been bringing their produce for sale each Wednesday for generations past. Wander down there if you happen to be at the *White Hart* on Market Day; it's well worth while.

Colchester is the next objective. To reach it you travel fifteen miles along the old Roman road from St. Albans, the Stane Street. At the end of it you find one of Rome's most important cities in England and the *Red Lion*, an inn built on the site of an important Roman dwelling. The earliest tale of the *Red Lion* is told in a portion of Roman mosaic pavement found beneath the inn and displayed there. For the next we must wait for some thirteen hundred years. That is told by fourteenth-century masonry and a stone doorway in the vaulted cellars which are believed to be survivals of a monkish building. In the hundred years that followed they built much of the *Red Lion* that stands to-day.

A lot has been written about this museum specimen of old inns. The student will find it described technically in the Essex volume Reports of the Historical Monuments Commission where accounts of several of the other inns referred to in this chapter will also be found. But to put it briefly the *Red Lion* consists of the original two-storied hall of timber and wattle and daub erected about 1470, with extensive very early sixteenth-century additions and further additions and enlargements made during the subsequent years. The 1470 portion is to the right beyond the entrance archway. This is generally accepted to have been built as a private dwelling-house for some rich burgess or merchant at the time of the Wars of the

Roses and twenty-two years before Columbus set out for America.

The block facing the street was erected, or materially enlarged, a few years later; about 1500 the experts say, at which time the house was converted to an inn. Thence onward the story of the house is told in timber and plaster and brick, and the records of the town. The rare architectural details of the grand old place are so many that they should be taken slowly to be appreciated. Wherever you go you find magnificent oak, and carving and tracery work. The George and Dragon on the spandrels of the entrance archway were carved in Henry VII.'s reign. The finely moulded ceiling beams of the Grill Room are even older. This room, by the way, has only recently been restored; for years, perhaps centuries, it was in use as the inn kitchen. The timber work in the Dining-room, where there is a good King Post to the roof, is also of the older, original house. On the first floor landing what appears to be a screen is the survival of a four-light Gothic window that once looked out upon a fifteenth-century world. The carved traceried panels on the front of the house are of very early craftsmanship. The Oak Lounge upstairs has beautifully moulded beams. And yet this marvellous timber was hidden for generations. The King Post was only uncovered in 1927. In the coaching days such decoration was counted old-fashioned and if not to be destroyed, to be hidden from view. Happily at the *Red Lion* it was only hidden.

As an inn, the house is mentioned in records of 1515. An "Auncyent Inne" it is called in 1604 when it was licensed as a "Wyn taverne." Many years earlier the city fathers ordained that "the pease and roote market, with the onions, garlick and cucumbers, shall be holden and kept from the *Lyon* sign downward towards St. Nicholas church and in no other place."

This suggests that the *Red Lion* existed before most of the ale-houses which so exercised the concern of the town's rulers towards the end of the sixteenth century. In December, 1598, some strong remarks were made by the Colchester Town Assembly respecting "the multitude of alehouses which have been suffered to be kept within the town of Colchester," some being denounced as "harbourers of Theves . . . and other lewd persones." And it was alleged that the "auncyent Boroughe" was thereby discredited to the "utter undoeinge of many of the poor inhabitants, and the same their wives and children." It was ordered that the inns and taverns should be restricted and only licensed houses permitted. The introduction of licensing, however, was not intended to discourage the drinking of ale. Indeed, the price was to be kept down and the quality raised—the price was three pints for a penny!

One of the early road coaches plied from the *Red Lion* to London, in 1756. But although always a busy posting inn in later years, the Mails and the important coaches used the *Three Cups* as a stopping-place. The old courtyard is attractive, with the inn's old room bells still hanging, and on a small rain-water cistern, bearing the date 1716, and the initials T. G. (probably a reminder of Thomas Gibson, a former landlord), is a Red Lion, crowned, and holding a sceptre surmounted with a fleur-de-lys. In 1515 the inn is recorded as "le Whyght Lyon, the garden of the Earl of Surrey belonging to the hostelry *Albi Leonis*." This Earl of Surrey was son of the general at Flodden (1513) and one would think the lion changed colour after Flodden; but it is recorded as the *White Lyon* until 1604 and probably became red on the accession of James I. to commemorate the union of the crowns.

The *Red Lion* has had many famous landlords who have been traced back without a break to 1758. Of the earlier ones perhaps the most notable are Rich and his successor, Richard Boyse. In 1656 Rich issued a trade token which was evidence of the inn's import-ance, and in 1668 his successor issued another, a specimen of which is preserved at the inn.

It is interesting to see the sort of coaching trade the *Red Lion* was carrying on in the middle of the eighteenth century. In February, 1756, an advertisement in the *Ipswich Journal* states that: "James Unwin, late coachman to Mr. Hills in Colchester, begs to inform the Publick that on Thursday, 9th March, he sets out from the Red Lyon Inn at Colchester, with a STAGE CART and able horses, to be at the Bell Inn at Leadenhall Street, London, on Wednes-day by one o'clock."

This was the customary cheap or third-class way of getting to London at that time. But the *Red Lion* also catered for the first-class passenger. This is an advertisement in the same journal in 1761:

*This is to give notice*

That on Monday, the 11th instant, will set out the FAREWELL POST-CHAISE with good horses and careful Drivers, from the following Inns at sixpence per mile from London to Colchester, and from Colchester to London in 8 hours. To set out from the RED LYON at Colchester at Seven, and from the GREEN DRAGON in Whitechapel, London, at Eight every morning in the week, for the more quick and easy convenience of such as do not choose travelling in Stage Coaches.

Thus the fare from Colchester to London (51 miles) was 25s.6d. in luxury as compared with the stage coach fare of 14s. insides and 7s. outsides.

The *Red Lion*'s rival in the Posting Age was the *Cups* across the road to the left. The *Three Cups* it used to be called, and despite its modern appearance it has a three-hundred-and-sixty-year-old pedigree, and some tales to tell. Behind its fifty-odd-year-old front remains much of a house rebuilt in the very early years of the nineteenth century when the *Cups* was the "Head Inn" of the town.

To get a true sense of contrast between the luxury room of 1500 and that of 1800 you have but to walk from the Grill Room of the *Red Lion* to the Dining-room of the *Cups*. Each was the best of its age. At the *Cups* you find a spacious chamber in the Renaissance style that was newly opened in 1807 when Louis XVIII. of France visited the inn. "The Elegant Large new Room" it was described in local newspapers at that time, and it had been built as the great Assembly and Ball Room of Colchester. It is still an elegant and remarkable chamber. Its Musicians' Gallery, entered through a trap-door in the corridor above, has a delightful railing with harp design in the centre, and there are other details to please the lover of the taste of those times.

The *Red Lion* is mediæval, the *Cups* is purely Georgian in atmosphere. The list of distinguished visitors to the inn in coaching days is a long one. George IV. was entertained here in 1817, and four years later, when the body of his unhappy and neglected Queen Caroline was being taken to Harwich on its way to burial in Brunswick, there is record that her coffin was left unguarded in the High Street on a hot August day while the escort spent some time in the *Cups*, in refreshment.

The Elegant "Large new Room" of the *Cups* for all its age and history seems curiously modern after the hoary antiquity of the *Red Lion*, but it is well to preserve a sense of proportion in the study of old inns. Every age has its own tales to tell and the oldest are not necessarily the best, nor the easiest understood. There is something very grim about the thought of that thirsty escort drinking at the *Cups*, while a Queen of England's body rested, uncared for, in the hot street outside.

You may spend many profitable days in Colchester, where Rome seems so much nearer than in any other English town, and when you leave it to pick up the tales of English inns again there is a choice of routes. You may go eighteen miles on to Ipswich and begin wandering among the fine old inns of Suffolk and Norfolk, or you may turn back to London. Whichever the choice may be, see the *Blue Boar* at Maldon first.

Maldon is seventeen miles away, an ancient little seaport town at the head of a tidal river. About six miles along the road is pleasant sounding Layer Marney, where, if you are wise, you will turn aside to visit Layer Marney Tower, a mile and a half to your left. The Tower is a magnificent Tudor brick building, seventy feet high, the Gatehouse of an unfinished mansion begun in the early sixteenth century, by Sir Henry Marney, privy counsellor to Henry VIII. Go into the church and see the Marney tombs, then turn back to your road and make for the *Blue Boar*, a very, very old inn, parts of which are older even than the *Red Lion*.

At first glance you would never suspect this. Viewed from the street the *Blue Boar* shows a sombre, grey brick front put up little more than a hundred years ago. It is in the courtyard through the archway that the old, half-timber work is seen, and in the long, left-hand wing, on the authority of the Historical Monuments Commission, is a timber and plaster wall that was built in the 1300's. This wall, pierced by two doorways of the same date, is thought to have originally been a screen at the end of a one-storied hall. The rest of this wing is a hundred years later and in it you see a little-altered building of the fifteenth century, rich in moulded beams and iron-hard roof and wall timbers.

In the yard is one of the rough mounting blocks our forefathers used to help them into the saddle. You often find these surviving in old inn yards, though sometimes put to other uses or thrust away into some corner by a generation that has forgotten their purpose.

The main part of the house, facing the street, is more modern, though its coffee-room is panelled from floor to ceiling in Jacobean oak, most of it found *in situ*. But the other rooms have more the air of the Georgians. The "Long Room" used for assemblies is in its conventional position on the first floor at the front. It is now divided into bedrooms. The Drawing Room with its pleasing eighteenth-century carved wood mantelpiece was the ante-chamber of the Assembly Room. There is painted pine panelling in some of the other rooms and a good deal of old furniture has been left in the inn. Some years ago, in stripping layers of paper from a wall at the *Blue Boar*, a locked cupboard was found in the panelling behind and in it some old drinking glasses.

The *Blue Boar's* sign was taken from a badge of the feudal family of De Vere, Earls of Oxford, whose Essex home was at Hedingham Castle, twenty miles inland. Local history claims that the inn was originally a dwelling-house of the De Veres, but it had become an inn at the sign of the "blewe bore" by 1573, and it has remained in business ever since.

All Saints church immediately opposite is notable for its triangular tower, the only one in England, and it has a particular interest for American visitors, for in its churchyard in January, 1652, Lawrence Washington, great-great-grandfather of George Washington, was buried.

The road back to London from Maldon runs through Danbury, one of the highest parishes in this flat county of Essex—it is 365 feet above sea-level—and on to the main road at Chelmsford. If this be your way and you feel adventurous, mark Purfleet by the Thames bank on your map, turn left at Brentwood, and make for it.

Purfleet really belongs to London now. All about it are old chalk quarries and factories and wharves, but the *Royal Hotel* there, not old, a hundred years at the most perhaps, has a particular

*The* Bull *at Long Melford, another inn where the original front has been restored. It was built as a cloth merchant's house about 1450.*

(See Chapter 3)

*The* Bell *at Thetford. Its corner post is thickly studded with nails.*
*Public proclamations were fastened to it in old days.*

(See Chapter 3)

*The* Duke's Head *at King's Lynn, built "for the accommodation
of merchants resorting to the Exchange".*
(See Chapter 3)

*The* Swan *at Harleston, an early eighteenth century rebuilding of a sixteenth century inn with some fine wrought ironwork supporting its sign.*
(See Chapter 3)

charm. The *Royal Hotel* was formerly known as the *Purfleet Hotel*, later as *Wingrove's*, and some writers say it once bore the prosaic sign of the *Bricklayers' Arms*. But that doesn't matter. The charm of the house is that it stands by the side of the Thames, and from its wide balconies you may look across three-quarters of a mile of "London River" to the Kentish hills, and watch ships from all the world passing up and downstream, as it seems but a stone's throw away.

The *Royal* was one of the Thames-side inns famed for its white-bait meals in our grandparents' days. Half a century ago it was a popular lunching place on Sundays of the theatrical world of London. They say that Edward VII. when Prince of Wales often honoured the house, *incognito*, with his patronage, and that Parnell and Mrs. O'Shea frequently lunched there. This inn is a real Victorian relic of those quieter prosperous days of the last century. And a seafaring inn too, for it is much used by ship's officers from vessels at the wharves and docks near by.

It is probably the successor of a riverside tavern, rebuilt to cater for traffic along one of the newer roads to Tilbury at the end of the Coaching Era. But it is an inn of character, well built in the taste of its time and a house to be visited by those who love ships as well as inns. The road to London is dreary and tiresome, undeniably, and really the simplest way to reach the *Royal* is by Green Line bus from Aldgate. And if you choose a good day you can sit on the balcony for hours watching the big and little steamers, the Thames barges and the fussy little tug boats, passing by and never know a dull moment.

The *Royal* at Purfleet fits oddly into this chapter, but then it is an odd inn. That must be its justification.

# CHAPTER THREE

## In Suffolk and Norfolk

ONE OF the best-known inns in England is the *Great White Horse* at Ipswich. That is because Charles Dickens chose to make it the scene of Mr. Pickwick's embarrassing adventure with "the middle-aged lady in yellow curl papers." So, to every lover of Pickwick, the *Great White Horse* is a shrine.

An ugly, grey-brick box of a place, its present front materially altered in the year 1818, it yet retains to-day much of the character of the inn at which young Mr. Dickens stayed in 1835.

"An inn known far and wide by the appellation of the *Great White Horse*," he described it, "rendered the more conspicuous by a stone statue of some rampacious animal . . . distantly resembling an insane cart horse which is elevated above the principal door."

For a wonder he disliked the place; he liked most inns of which he wrote. "A corpulent man, with a fortnight's napkin under his arm and coeval stockings on his legs," may have received him uncivilly at the door, as he received Mr. Pickwick. Perhaps Mr. Dickens had to wait an hour for "a bit of fish and a steak," and "a bottle of the worst possible port wine" as Mr. Pickwick and Mr. Peter Magnus did.

Mr. Dickens would think better of the inn now, but he would still see a large white horse elevated above the principal door, and still find the labyrinths of passages and clusters of rooms collected together between the four walls of the inn, of which he told, though they are no longer uncarpeted, or mouldy or badly lighted.

Of course the great sight of the house is the "Pickwick Room," furnished in period, with a couple of four-poster beds and resembling closely the chamber described in the immortal *Pickwick Papers* in which, blushing with shame, poor Mr. Pickwick unwittingly observed the middle-aged lady brushing her back hair. One should always read the twenty-second chapter of *Pickwick* before visiting the *Great White Horse*.

But the inn has a history going far, far beyond the days of Dickens. There was a *White Horse* standing here in 1518 that was counted the first inn of the town, and the little stretch of oak-timbered wall with a blocked-up window that you see in the present modernised Lounge is probably a survival of that building. The Lounge was a courtyard then, into which you drove through a gateway where the present main door stands.

King George II. was at the *Great White Horse* in 1737, stopping on his way from Lowestoft to London and receiving, although it was eleven o'clock of a January night, the dignitaries of the town in the Great Dining-room upstairs. Another King, Louis XVIII. of France, was entertained there, and Lord Nelson spent a night at the inn in 1800. But then practically everybody who journeyed along the East Anglian highway in the Posting Era knew the bustling *Great White Horse*, as nearly everybody does to-day.

From Ipswich, if you take the road through Hadleigh you come quickly upon some of the most delightful country in Suffolk; sleepily peaceful, utterly unspoiled. You pass villages, as lovely as their names, Monks Eleigh and Brent Eleigh, and reach in eighteen miles the Tudor town of Lavenham, one of the rarest places in all England. You will do well to swing a mile out of your way to pass through Kersey, which claims to be the prettiest village in Suffolk, and if you are wise find your way back to your road through adjoining Lindsey, and, pondering their names, realise that you are in England's old weaving country, the villages of which gave names to cloth that we use to this day.

Lavenham was a prosperous weaving town in the fifteenth and sixteenth centuries. Its blue cloth was famous throughout Europe, and its immensely rich merchants built the magnificent timbered houses and the Wool Hall and the Guildhall which happily still remain. Lavenham is extraordinarily rich in these old timbered buildings, and one of the oldest, at the corner of High Street and Water Street, is the *Swan* inn.

At the age of the inn it is hard to guess exactly, but much of it must have been built when men were alive who fought in the

Wars of the Roses, and although it has been altered from time to time in the intervening years it has not been spoiled. If you look at its Water Street front you see remains of early moulded decoration on the plaster work; a fleur-de-lys, surmounted by a Crown and a Tudor Rose. If you go into the picturesque yard you see an outside door to an upstairs room. Through this door woollen cloth was unloaded from the open gallery where the weavers sat, on to the wagon waiting in the yard below. The first floor of the long wing to the right above the Bar was once an open gallery; you will find traces of it inside.

The *Swan* in Charles II.'s reign was important enough for a landlord, John Girling, to issue his own Trade Token under the sign of the house. That was in 1667, and sixty-five years later the first travellers' guide to Suffolk measured the road distances to the *Swan*. In the Bar of this old inn hang a peal of sweet-toned handbells. These were used by the church bell-ringers up to a few years ago for a weekly practice in the bar.

Lavenham is a town with which time has dealt very kindly. Its streets have delightful names—Lady Street, Prentice Street, Bear Lane, Shilling Street are some of them. And in a four-hundred-year-old house in Shilling Street one Jane Taylor in the early nineteenth century wrote poems for children, one of which: "Twinkle, twinkle, little star" is known the English speaking world over.

Only four or five miles from Lavenham—you go out past its great upstanding church—you come to another very ancient inn, the *Bull* at Long Melford, built, so the experts say, about 1450. The *Bull* was not always an inn. It began as the mansion of some rich clothier or cloth maker for, like Lavenham, Long Melford was a weaving town in the latter Middle Ages, and it was for him that these massive timbers and curious carvings were erected and made. Out at the back where the inn-yard came to be were his workshops and looms.

There is some interesting carving to be found in this house. Just inside the door of the hall or Lounge is a representation of that mysterious creature the "wood-wose" or "wild man," that figures in both church and domestic decoration, concerning the explanation of which the antiquaries have long argued. High up on the side of the house looking on to Bull Lane is a charming little two-light traceried Gothic window that may first have lighted the old wool-man's "Solar Chamber" or "Parlour." But wherever you wander in the *Bull* you find timber work, most of which must date from Elizabeth's reign, at the latest.

The house has been in use as an inn certainly since 1570. The family of Drew, which held the *Bull* in the sixteen hundreds, has left its initials "W.D." and "A.E.D." on the two carved posts on either side of the entrance door. The date 1649 probably records some alteration made at that time. One of the posts was hidden for years and only came to light during recent restoration. Even the timber front of the *Bull* was screened for a century or more behind an ugly flat brick wall, and the fine timber work of the Saloon Bar has only lately been uncovered. The yard is a picturesque place, once surrounded by open galleries, which, as at Lavenham, you may easily trace.

One of the many stories the *Bull* could tell is that of a brawl in its entrance hall when Richard Evered, a well-to-do Melford yeoman, was attacked and killed. That was in July, 1648, in the troubled days of the Civil War. They took Evered's assailant, tried him and hanged him, and Evered lies buried in Melford's beautiful church across the common.

If you love old buildings you must visit this church. Its Lady Chapel is a joy and the church contains much glorious old stained glass. You should see, also, before you leave, Melford's two great Tudor Mansions, Melford Hall close by the *Bull*, and moated Kent-well Hall beyond the church. Then take the road northward to Bury St. Edmunds thirteen miles away.

The *Suffolk Hotel* here is a modern-looking place that was largely rebuilt about a century ago and has had its simple front marred in comparatively recent times by new building of the ground floor. But the *Suffolk* has a long history. It was called the *Greyhound* for centuries and once belonged to the Abbey of St. Edmund at Bury. There are records of a house on the site in 1295, and it was an inn and known as "*le Greyhounde*" when the Abbey surrendered its property in 1539. There is little of the old fabric left, and most of that is below ground, but one curious thing about this house is its hidden rooms, closed up in the course of the early nineteenth-century reconstruction, why, who can say? One, a pantry, was discovered a few years ago when they were running hot-water pipes through the house. It was examined through the floor of No. 15 room and closed again. There is said to be another hidden and forgotten room at the back overlooking High Baxter Street, but there is no doubt about the abandoned pantry.

Our next stop is Thetford. There is a direct road, or you can be more enterprising and go by way of Newmarket—those coming up from Cambridge will join our route through this great racing town. Here was the *White Hart*, an old inn once worth visiting. It suffered severely at the hands of German raiders. In the old days it shared the fortunes of the racing world it served and had many tales to tell of great personages, big wagers and famous wins. It is worth recalling still because of an ancient custom. Every year, for over a century, the "Felon's Dinner" was held here in the last week in March. This custom began in the eighteen-twenties with the annual meeting of a society formed to pursue and prosecute poachers and similar evil-doers in the neighbourhood.

As the racehorse is lord of this pleasant town, so he is lord of the breezy heathland round about. And it is across these heathlands that the road leads to Thetford—a grand road for motoring, dead straight for miles. But our posting and coaching ancestors feared the desolation of the wild Newmarket heaths, for they provided too happy a hunting ground for the "Gentlemen of the Road." The tale of highway robbery between Newmarket and Thetford in the old days is a long and full one.

You reach Thetford at the end of a twenty-mile journey from Newmarket and you come again to a border town. Part in Norfolk, part in Suffolk, the peaceful river Little Ouse divides the counties shortly before you reach the *Bell* at the corner of the London road and King Street. Before you enter the inn look carefully at its historic corner post at the angle of those two highways. This massive timber is thickly studded with nails, and those nails tell of public proclamations fastened there in bygone days when the "Bell Corner Post" was the customary place on which to display all local, official notices.

The *Bell's* recorded history starts in 1493 when it was the property of the College of the Virgin Mary in Thetford, and that wing to which the corner post belongs is the oldest part. When you look at the front to King Street, with its sturdy oak timbers, silver-grey with age, you look at a building that was standing when Columbus sailed for America. When you explore that wing you may find rare relics of the art and craftmanship of Tudor workmen. The walls of some of the upper rooms were painted in Queen Elizabeth's days and some of this painting was uncovered in 1938 and has been preserved. At the same time a little Tudor fireplace was discovered in a bedroom. The wall paintings seem to have been covered up in the late sixteen hundreds, for in front of them was stretched a linen, cotton and wool fabric of that date upon which wallpapers had subsequently been pasted. In 1948 a wattle and daub wall was uncovered which dates probably from the end of the fifteenth century.

At the *Bell* there is a good example of the once open gallery that was approached from and looked on to the courtyard. It runs at the back of the old wing, and the staircase by which you reach it, originally led from the yard itself.

Thetford is an interesting old place steeped in history. It had twenty churches once and was the capital of East Anglia and the city of its kings. Six miles away, at Brandon, survives one of the oldest crafts in the world, the craft of flint knapping. They still make gun flints there as they made flint arrow-heads and axes for the Stone Age man. You should visit Brandon, then turn north again, through the biggest of the new State Forests of England, and make for the town of Merchant Princes, King's Lynn, thirty-two miles distant.

The *Duke's Head*, which is your inn here, is a very fine example of late seventeenth-century architecture, built for a wealthy vintner of the town, Sir John Turner, in 1685, the last year of Charles II.'s reign.

The duke, whose head gives the sign to this inn, was probably the Duke of York, who as James II. succeeded Charles. Sir John Turner opened his new house under that sign, on the site of an older inn called the *Griffin* which he had bought two years previously. As local history tells, Sir John built the *Duke's Head*, "for the accommodation of merchants resorting to the Exchange," for Lynn in those days was a bustling, prosperous port engaged in the wine and Baltic trades and the Greenland Fishery, and the Exchange was the delightful little Custom House that still stands on the quay.

Sir John employed a fellow-townsman, Henry Bell, to build his great new inn in the Tuesday Market Place. Bell was the architect of the Exchange and his work has sometimes been compared with that of Sir Christopher Wren. He built the house of brick, which has since been defaced with plaster, and there is a fine moulded-panelled Lounge with two charming contemporary wooden mantel-pieces.

At one time the principal rooms of the inn were known by individual names. There were the " Wainscot Room," which maybe is now the Lounge; the " Great Parlour," the " Hare," the " Partridge" and the " Cock-fighting" rooms. Tradition says that the inn in its earlier days offered no welcome to the common traveller who came by coach. He must arrive in his own carriage, or a chaise at least, to be wanted at the *Duke's Head*. But those days passed and it became the " Head" coaching inn of the town. And in later days still it entertained King Edward VII. as Prince of Wales in the Masonic Lodge which has met there for many years past.

King's Lynn is full of history and relics of its prosperous past. Royalty is often seen shopping in its narrow streets, for it is Sandringham's market town. It claims among its more famous sons Vancouver, explorer of North America, and Eugene Aram, sometime usher at its Grammar School, went out from Lynn " with gyves upon his wrists."

You go out from Lynn by the Norwich road, journeying for just over forty miles through a peaceful, agricultural land, until you reach Norwich. At East Dereham, twenty-seven miles on your way, the poet Cowper lies buried in the church, and George Borrow was born at Dumpling Green a mile to the south. Perhaps you will break your journey for half an hour to pay a pilgrimage to their shrines, but when you come to Norwich, make for the *Bell* on Orford Hill, under the shadow of the great Norman castle keep.

As the *Blue Bell* this inn was known in other days, and Orford Hill was known as Hog Hill, and the *Blue Bell* was in business

*The Yard of the* White Lion *at Eye, an ancient inn that has never been restored. Its fine Georgian Assembly Room is shown below.*

(See Chapter 3)

*A Tudor inn in a Tudor town. The* Swan *at Lavenham is an excellent example of the uncovering of the original front of an old inn.*
(See Chapter 3)

*The* Crown and Castle *at Orford with the old Norman Keep
in the background.*
(See Chapter 3)

*A wayside inn on a by-pass road made in the 1820's. The* Green Dragon
*between Barnet and South Mimms.*

(See Chapter 4)

before 1600. It was never a popular posting house, but rather the inn of the county, the farmers who came to the adjoining market, and of the citizens of Norwich itself.

Its exterior is not prepossessing, but inside you will find survivals of the craftsmanship of nearly four centuries. There are carved oak beams of Elizabethan date, a pleasing Georgian staircase, additions of Queen Victoria's days and a spice of frank modernity. All of which goes to make up a very attractive inn. Once more you will find an old gallery, long since glazed, looking down upon the glass roof of the entrance hall which was once the *Blue Bell's* courtyard.

The *Bell* was a popular cock-fighting inn a couple of hundred years ago. One advertisement, published in 1725, invites patrons to attend a great cock match "to show thirty-one cocks on a side, for two guineas a cock and twenty guineas the odd battle," adding, "Gentlemen shall be accommodated with a glass of excellent wine and care taken to prevent disturbance by the mob."

Sam Barker, a landlord thirty years later, also appreciated the uses of advertisement. He advertised the then comparatively new malt liquor, porter. "A truly British liquor," he called it, of which he had "a large quantity always bottled and fit to drink." He offered it at five shillings a dozen (thirteen bottles to the dozen) or three shillings if you returned the bottles.

It was in Sam Barker's time that the "Hell Fire Club" met at the *Bell*. The "Hell Fire Club" appears to have been composed of rowdies. They called themselves "Gentlemen of Principles," but their chief object seems to have been to persecute the Methodists and break up meetings of John and Charles Wesley when they preached in the city. Later, the *Bell* housed the "Original Club," or Communists as we might call them now, who lauded the French Revolutionaries and advocated revolution in this country.

But the *Bell* swung to the "right" in later years still. "The Loyal and Constitutional Club" was founded there in 1831, with the Duke of Wellington among its original members. Its old Minute Books are preserved in the house to prove that the ancient inn had renounced its earlier wild ways and had become quite respectable.

From Norwich take the Bungay road southward, and if you

T.O.I.                                                                                    D want to linger on your way turn right in about four miles and visit Caister St. Edmunds which was a flourishing town of far greater importance than Norwich in Roman days. The parish church stands within the Roman walls, and if you are lucky you may find excavators at work and see something of what they have uncovered of this very old Norfolk town. Then back to your main road, past Ditchingham Park, where Sir Rider Haggard lived and wrote, and so into quaint Bungay. Then turn right, along the Waveney valley, the border of Norfolk and Suffolk, and come in twenty-two and a half miles from Norwich to the *Swan* at Harleston.

Its fine sign, and the beautiful wrought-iron bracket from which it hangs, are well worthy of notice, so is the well-proportioned mellow brick front of the block that faces the main street. This is a rebuilding of the very early Georgian days, for the *Swan* dates from 1551 when youthful Edward VI. was King of England. You find remains of the original inn at the back, in the two wings that enclose the *Swan's* picturesque courtyard.

One Robert Cook built the place, and he may be counted a lucky man, for only a year or two before he had been a rebel, concerned in Kett's rising that sent many a Norfolk man to the scaffold. But Cook was pardoned for his " treasons and misprisions of treasons" and built the *Swan*, and one hopes lived lawfully and happily in Harleston to the end of his days with tales to tell of Kett's Rebellion of 1549, that we should dearly love to hear now.

The old part of the inn is mostly given up to kitchens and larders; it is in the main block that you find the more interesting rooms. Here is the old Assembly Room—the "Long Room" as it is so often called in eighteenth-century inns—where the big social and political functions of the town were held. It is panelled throughout in the early Georgian style, with, as was traditional in these "Long Rooms," a window giving access to the top of the porch of the entrance doorway. From the top of the porch political candidates would address their constituents in the street below, and famous visitors show themselves to the cheering people. The iron railings of this particular porch are a fine example of the eighteenth-century blacksmith's craft.

Flanking the Assembly Room are smaller chambers with some

panelling, now bedrooms but formerly ante-rooms to the big chamber. A big window, overlooking the yard in the corridor on the first floor, is said to have served a different purpose from that odd first floor door at Lavenham. Through it luggage was unloaded from the coach's roof; a simple labour-saving device of our ancestors in the days before lifts. Beyond the yard is a big kitchen garden.

Among the *Swan's* past landlords was one with the unusual name of Joel Dissenmers. He bought the inn in 1670. Jonathan Nobbs was landlord a hundred years ago, and in his time the *Swan* was the headquarters of a flourishing savings bank of 600 depositors with £15,000 to their credit. A nineteenth-century landlord, Neal Young-man, was one of the biggest wine merchants in the neighbourhood.

The *Swan* at Harleston is an unusually charming example of the early coaching inn and so little had change affected it that until recently it had no big Coffee Room. For the public Dining-room or Coffee Room is a comparatively modern innovation. Your old-time traveller took his meals in a private parlour or in the kitchen, according to his means and tastes.

From Harleston, make your way to Eye, another sleepy, forgotten little East Anglian town twelve miles away. You have a choice of routes. The better road is westward to Scole, where the famous *Great Inn of Scole*, built in the mid-seventeenth century, still stands by the side of the Norwich turnpike. Turn towards Ipswich there and, in a couple of miles, left at Broome. The other route is for the adventurous. You take the Weybread road out of Harleston, quickly cross the Waveney and re-enter Suffolk. And then—read your map. You will wind and wander through quiet little roads, barely more than wide lanes. If you lose your way and happen upon Wingfield, the sight of a moated castle there will compensate you. And when at last you come to Eye stop at the church and see its magnificent painted screen. Then make for the *White Lion*.

Do not be misled by its rather ordinary front. Behind that, with the exception of a Georgian brick addition at the rear, there is little that was built after Queen Elizabeth died and some moulded beams that were in place before she was born. Go through the archway into the yard and look back. You will see as charmingly delightful a medley of old roof and wall as you can wish for.

The *White Lion* has never been restored. Some of its old beams are exposed, but you can guess what a wealth of ancient timber is hidden in the house by the bulges in wall and ceiling that proclaim great beams behind the wallpaper and plaster. And many of the grates must be set in once open hearths that may one day be open again. The varying roof levels make it obvious that the inn is made up of several houses, all of them old. There is a moulded rafter in the scullery ceiling that looks like fifteenth-century work, work of the earliest Tudors, anyhow.

But perhaps the most interesting room in the place is its charming little mid-eighteenth-century Assembly or Ball Room. This is in the Adam style, decorated in white and gold, with at one end a queer little Musicians' Gallery approached by a ladder. Above the dignified mantelpiece are framed the arms of the Kerrison family, closely associated with the town for many years, and here for nearly two centuries Eye has danced and held its big dinners and parties, and routs. The *Suffolk Chronicle* of just over a hundred years ago reports a function here, after a review of the County Yeomanry, when: "a retreat was made to the *White Lion* where dinner was provided at 2s. 6d. a head, including as much wine and punch as each man could swallow." There is record of a book published in 1817, the title page of which reads: "A Dialogue between M.N. and O. wrote by a Suffolk Ploughboy . . . began on the 27th day of September, 1817, and wrote at *White Lion* Eye Suffolk." The dialogue is a rambling one dealing with the making of a canal from Yarmouth to Diss.

When the *White Lion* was built it stood in the Market Place, though for nearly a hundred years past its address has been Broad Street, which implies that in the old days there were no houses opposite and that it faced a wide Market Square. "Noller's Vans" plying between Norwich and London called here three times a week when the last century was young. These vans carried both passengers and merchandise, travelled slowly, and their charges were far lower than those of the coaches. Behind the old stables in the yard is the bowling green which still draws players to the inn on summer evenings as it has done for generations past.

You will leave ancient Eye, the name of which means "island,"

and the venerable *White Lion* with reluctance. Your way now runs through fourteen miles of utterly unspoiled rural England, by little roads that twist and wind, and through sleepy forgotten villages. Unless you read your map carefully you may get off our road now and again; but you are in good country in which to lose your way. Sooner or later you will find a sign-post pointing to Framlingham and presently see in the distance the towers of Framlingham's ancient castle walls, and come at last to the Market Hill and the *Crown*.

The *Crown* is a fine old Posting Inn with a noble sign above it, for very many years the centre of the life of its serene little town. Petty Sessions for thirty-three parishes were held here weekly in mid-Victorian days, and they built a Corn Hall in its yard in 1847, but with the decline of Framlingham as a market town it became obsolete and has been made into extra bedrooms.

The inn is a very old one, and you will find the workmanship of many ages within. Most of the oak rafters and wall beams were put in place by Tudor craftsmen and remained hidden beneath the plaster of a later age until revealed by restoration work carried out during 1951-52. In the bar and lounge may be seen sections of wattle and daub wall, of the type used in the sixteenth century. The archway which once led from Market Hill to the yard has now been filled in, but in the entrance hall you walk on the great stone slabs of the driveway over which coaches once rattled. There is a graceful early eighteenth century staircase, broad and shallow-stepped, with charming balusters leading from the entrance to the corridors of the upper floor. At the top are the doors of the conventional "Long Room," where in 1803 gentlemen of the neighbourhood enrolled in the "Yeomanry Cavalry": here the balls and banquets of the town were held, and during 1834 Subscription Card Parties cheered many a long winter's evening.

Since its restoration the *Crown* shows something of the beauty of the inn that was standing in 1553 when an army of 13,000 men rallied at Framlingham in support of Princess Mary, soon to become Queen Mary, who had taken refuge in the castle during the brief reign of the ill-fated Lady Jane Grey. Those summer days were exciting and stirring ones for Framlingham. You should see the castle before you leave, though only its outer walls remain. The rest was pulled down in the early sixteen hundreds and a century later the great space within the walls was a favourite arena for prize-fights. And you should visit the unusually beautiful tombs of the Howards, Dukes of Norfolk, in the Church. Then journey seven miles to the *Bell* at Saxmundham.

When first you see this severely plain grey-brick house you may wonder at its place among old inns. But to a lover of inns it is an example of peculiar interest. It is a genuine coaching inn, perhaps the last ever erected for that purpose. It was built in 1842, fourteen years before the railway came to Saxmundham, and it embodied the last word in comfort for the road travellers of the time. In design it copied the traditional features of the older coaching inns. Until recently it had its bar in the entrance hall where the office is now. It has a "Long Room" on the first floor over the entrance porch. At the back were an extensive garden, a bowling green and a spacious stableyard. And in that yard the "Old Blue," a famous East Suffolk coach that called daily at the *Bell* to the very last, lay derelict for years and was at length broken up there. The echo of the coach horn seems very near at the *Bell* at Saxmundham.

Of the old inn that was pulled down to make place for the present one there are some remains in the cellars where massive walls of early brickwork tell of Tudor days. The *Bell* was always an important inn on the Great Yarmouth road. George II. rested there in January, 1737, and Lord Stafford sent a special team of horses to draw the royal carriage on its way. It took the king four hours to travel the twenty miles to the *Great White Horse* at Ipswich. That was on the occasion when he received the Ipswich city fathers at that inn.

We follow the same road, breaking our journey, as possibly King George did, at the *Crown* at Woodbridge, twelve miles on the way. The *Crown* is only about half the size that it was in the coaching days when it included the adjoining building in the main street. It is a fascinating old place with a very long history, and recent restoration has uncovered much half-timbered work there and a big open hearth in the Dining-room. The house seems to have been reconstructed with taste towards the end of the eighteenth century, doubtless to meet the demands of the rapidly increasing number of travellers by chaise and coach and to offer modern accommodation more comfortable and "elegant" than that provided by the original building.

There are two attractive panelled rooms, one with deep window seats, on the ground floor, and above stairs, a more elaborately decorated chamber, now divided and in use as bedrooms, that must have been the inn's Assembly Room. The present "black and white" Dining-room appears once to have been a kitchen. There are hooks part way up the newly-opened fireplace that tell of hams and bacon suspended there to cure in the wood smoke that went up from the hearth.

Whether the *Crown* began life as an inn is uncertain. The antiquaries tell you that it was the principal tenement of the Manor of Woodbridge-Ufford and that the Manorial Courts were held there up until the last century. But it was an inn in 1532, when Robert Fox was landlord, and a local merchants' Exchange was in being there. In the following century, when Woodbridge had a thriving shipbuilding trade, Peter Pett, of the great family of Chatham and Deptford shipwrights, owned the inn. It was he, they say, who built the ship that brought Charles II. home from exile in 1660, and when Peter Pett married Catherine Cole, their wedding feast was held at the *Crown*.

The *Crown*, like the *Bell* at Saxmundham, kept its coaching trade almost to within living memory. Coaches were calling at the house in 1855 certainly. But the old yard archway has been closed recently to provide an entrance lounge and its long range of stables have been converted to garages, and again the old inn has been modernised to keep abreast of the demands of its customers, even as it was in George III.'s time when they built the new panelled rooms that we look upon now with such pleasure. For an inn must always be changing if it is to survive.

There is much to see in quaint Woodbridge. There is a jolly little sixteenth-century Shire Hall and, opposite it, the house where Edward FitzGerald, translator of Omar Khayyám lived for many years. FitzGerald lies buried at Boulge, three miles away and near his grave a rose bush grows and blooms, raised from seeds

brought from Persia, the land of Omar himself.  To the east is a
little-known district of wild heath and forest land where lonely
tidal rivers eat in from the sea.  And there, on the coast, is the forgotten little seaport of Orford with a magnificent Norman castle
keep.  This keep was built by Henry II. in 1165 and is perhaps the
most perfect of its kind in England.  Its two great chambers, with
kitchens and bedrooms leading from them, are immensely impressive.
It has a delightful little Norman chapel, a deep well and, beneath
the entrance steps, an airless dungeon.  From the battlements, a
glorious view of the surrounding country and the sea may be had.
Orford's church, too, is interesting because of its ruined tower,
which fell down on a May morning in 1830 "about quarter past
eight a.m., just after the man who tolled the 8 o'clock bell had
quitted the church," according to a contemporary record.

In the shadow of the castle keep is the *Crown and Castle*, an ancient
inn rebuilt in 1879 on the site of an older house and recently completely modernised.  There is some uncertainty about the length of
time an inn has stood on this site, but probably a tavern or alehouse
existed there since very early days.

Until recently it was believed that the present building entirely
replaced the seventeenth-century inn which is shown in old pictures.
During recent alterations two fireplaces were uncovered which are
part of the original house, as are the moulded ceiling beams in this
room, although the floor is now lower than the original.

The modernisation was carried out in 1879 when Sir Richard
Wallace, remembered by the Wallace Collection in London,
owned the Sudbourne Estate of which the *Crown and Castle* was
part.

The *Crown*, as it is known locally, became an inn of importance
about a hundred years ago, when the eighteenth-century Orford
Hotel, now a private house, was closed upon the death of the old
landlord, Robert Cooper.  His wife, Jane Cooper, took the business
to the *Crown*, which has carried on as the principal inn of the town
ever since.

Now, back to Ipswich, to the *Great White Horse*—for a drink or
a meal perhaps, or maybe for your bed for the night.  On your way,
take a look at the attractive sign of the *Crown and Anchor* which

*The* White Horse *at Hertingfordbury, said to have been a farmhouse*
*before it became an inn.*
(See Chapter 4)

*A village inn on a village green.* *The* Rose & Crown *at Tewin.*
(See Chapter 4)

The "Slate" upon which debts were chalked up in the Bar of the Rose & Crown, Tewin. (*Right*) The "Slate" open.
(See Chapter 4)

*The* Roebuck *at Broadwater, a four-hundred-year-old inn on the Great North Road.*

(See Chapter 4)

# CHAPTER FOUR

## *A Round of Hertfordshire Inns*

THE INN has ever been closely associated with the road and shared its fortunes. When the road was busy its inns prospered, when the road became neglected its inns faded and often died. And a new inn came always hard on the heels of the road-makers. The first inn in this land probably arose by the side of the first road the Romans made; the latest you may see to-day going up by the side of a yet uncompleted by-pass.

So in wandering in search of tales of old inns you will often be running into tales of old roads. Take for example the *Green Dragon* between Chipping Barnet and South Mimms.

A modest, isolated, little house this; hardly more than a wayside tavern and by no means ancient as we count old inns for it is not far advanced into its second century of existence. But its story is interesting. It was built by the side of what to-day we should call a by-pass, constructed in the eighteen twenties. Even now they call it the "New Road," though for a hundred years and more it has formed part of the main highway to Holyhead and the North-west.

Telford, the great road-maker of coaching days, designed this by-pass, to shorten a bad and narrow, winding stretch of the Holyhead road that ran from Hadley High Stone, or the Barnet Pillar as it was better known then, to South Mimms. At Kitts End, on that road, was a thriving wayside inn, the *Bull's Head*. When the New Road was opened and the posting and coaching traffic deserted the old road the *Bull's Head* sickened and died and the *Green Dragon* arose on the New Road to take its trade. That was somewhere about 1830.

The *Green Dragon* is not pretentious. But it prospered and remained in the same family until it passed to its present control. The grandson of the man for whom the inn was built was the landlord when it changed hands. His mother, who was born about

59

1820 and died at the age of 97, remembered playing in the rafters of the inn when it was being built, and there has been little material alteration in the place since it was new. The porch is an addition, and you can see where a later extension has been made at one side. But otherwise the little *Green Dragon* is a wayside inn that was as familiar to the mail and stage-coach passengers of a hundred years ago as it is to the passing motorist to-day.

Its sign was obviously taken from a place name, for there is a "Green Dragon End" marked close by on a map of 1720. An interesting link with the past, a short mile away at the entrance of Dyrham Park, is a gateway which, according to long standing tradition, was originally erected in London as a triumphal arch to celebrate the return of King Charles II. to his Restoration in 1660.

Only a few hundred yards beyond the *Green Dragon*, a turn to the right leads to the Great North Road. Follow it to Hatfield, turn right there and make your way to Hertingfordbury. Here, by the side of the old posting road from Reading to Cambridge, is the *White Horse*, and the *White Horse* is a bit of a puzzle.

They say locally that at one time it was a farmhouse and that the original *White Horse* occupied much humbler premises across the road. That tale may well be true. But whatever its early history may be it is a very charming old inn set just back from the road by the side of Panshanger Park, with horse trough, and a cut-out sign topping a post in front, as all proper roadside inns should have, and it contains some most interesting features. From its entrance hall a short Jacobean or possibly Elizabethan staircase, with heavy balusters, leads to the first floor. There is some Jacobean panelling on the walls of the hall, and there was more until a few years ago. The differing ceiling levels tell of the alterations in past times and the heavy oak beams to be seen in various parts of the house were put in place by men who worked in the fifteen hundreds.

The old place has been much altered in its time. The present front is Georgian, a brick addition of the eighteenth century that masks an original half-timber front, the beams of which were discovered during alterations made a few years ago. The entrance door is flanked by heavy moulded timbers that came perhaps from a ceiling when they altered the house and built the brick front.

The inn's present sign-board is modern, but its old one is preserved in the house, a fine old sign that had braved the weather for many a long year. There is a puzzling mingling of the sixteenth and eighteenth centuries in this old inn that is so reticent to tell its tales of perhaps four centuries.

When you leave it, make for Tewin, turning right at Cole Green a couple of miles on the way, and facing Tewin Lower Green, where the village fair used to be held, stands the *Rose and Crown*, a typical village inn, a couple of hundred years old perhaps, that has preserved a rare relic of other days.

This is the "Slate" upon which things "are put," as we still say. The slate hangs in the Public Bar, hinged like a door. On it, unpaid debts were chalked up upon the inner side and decently hidden—for a reasonable time at any rate. But if they were not then paid, they were scored on the outer side for all the world to see, a subtle method of applying pressure to the debtor which might prove effective in similar circumstances to-day.

What is now called the Saloon Bar of the *Rose and Crown* was the Tap Room not so many years since. Then curved, high-backed settles were set about its open hearth, and there are tales told in the neighbourhood of poached game hidden in the small cupboard to the right of the hearth. The tiled weather-board building in the yard, now converted to a garage and tea-room, was the inn's skittle alley. Skittles was a popular game at Tewin, especially at fair time. With this homely, unspoiled little inn and its cosy bars and attractive red and blue chequered brick front, time has dealt very kindly.

From it a pretty winding way leads in a few miles to the old coaching town of Welwyn where two great roads divide. Here the Nottingham, Leeds and Ripon coach road forks left from the Great North Road and there are inns to visit on both.

Follow the Great North Road first. Just over four miles on, where the road from Ware joins it at Broadwater, is the *Roebuck*, a red-roofed, many-gabled old house, with a green in front, that suggests a Maypole, in as satisfying a setting as the most romantic of inn-lovers could ask. An ancient road runs on either side and in such a position there must have been an inn since men first travelled along those roads.

Tradition says it was built in 1420 and much of the early rough timber work inside the house supports tradition to within a year or two. The Tap Room is one of the oldest parts. Here you can see a portion of an early outside wall enclosed by a subsequent, yet long ago enlargement. And the wall and ceiling timbers on one of the landings are other examples of very old work.

Although never a coaching inn, in the spacious days of the road, the *Roebuck* was a regular stopping-place to pick up or set down passengers by the numerous mails and stages that clattered along the Great North Road at all hours of the day and night. Record of one distinguished traveller who came to the house is preserved in a letter that hangs on its walls. It was written by Edward Bulwer, first Lord Lytton, better known as Bulwer-Lytton the novelist, to John Forster, friend and biographer of Charles Dickens. Forster was coming to stay at Knebworth Park. Knebworth close by is still the home of the Lyttons and the *Roebuck* belonged to the Lytton family for generations. Lytton wrote in November, 1836, advising Forster to travel by the "York Express" from the *Saracen's Head*, Snow Hill, or the York coach from the *White Horse*, Fetter Lane, adding:

"These coaches do not pass our lodge, but you must tell the coachman to set you down at the *Roebuck* public-house, Broadwater . . . I will send my phaeton for you."

It would have taken John Forster the best part of four hours to do the 29-mile journey from London in 1836. The motor car does it inside the hour now. The old inn has collected a number of interesting relics of the past to hang on its walls, among them horse pistols, a flail, a coach horn and a Roman horseshoe dug up in the neighbourhood, all suggestive of good tales of old days.

But we journey on, branching at Stevenage a couple of miles beyond the *Roebuck*, and join the Leeds road on the outskirts of Hitchin. Here, the *Sun* is one of the great coaching inns of the road.

There are records of the *Sun* in 1575 and Mr. Reginald Hine, the historian of Hitchin, believe that it might be fifty years older. In his *Story of the Sun Hotel* he has told a number of interesting tales of this ancient posting house. One of the queerest is that of three highwaymen who held up the *Sun* in 1772, bound and robbed William Marshall, the landlord, and his guests and escaped with the swag, impudently inscribing their initials and the date on two bricks at the right of the entry before they went. Only the bricks with the date remain.

The *Sun* was the inn of the Parliamentarians during the Civil Wars and lost much of its popularity at the Restoration when King Charles II. came into his own again. It was many a year before it lived down its reputation. But with the coming of the coaches to the roads the *Sun* began to prosper once more. One of the early stage-coaches ran regularly between the *Sun* and the *Greyhound* in Smithfield in 1741, and the old inn knew all the coaches of its road that succeeded.

It was in these early posting days that the *Sun* pulled down its original Tudor block to the street and built the present dignified one of, now, mellow brick pierced by the fine archway leading to the yard. The Assembly Room was added in 1770, but a lot of the earlier house remains in the right-hand wing at the back. You will find moulded oak timbers in several of the rooms, and an odd little "Secret Chamber" approached from a cupboard in one of the bedrooms, at an angle where the eighteenth-century work joins that of the Tudor builders. Why this little room was made the visitor must guess for himself. Obviously for some good reason, but the *Sun* cannot supply it.

The old inn has had an eventful and busy past. As long ago as 1600, the local justices' courts were held there: later the Archdeaconry Court met under its roof. It was the rallying place for the local Militia in times of emergency, and during the Jacobite Rising in 1745 the *Sun* was the place appointed for enrolling of men of North Hertfordshire to resist the Young Pretender's advancing army. In the posting days its large kitchens were kept ever busy supplying the demands of travellers, and all the big dinners and balls of the neighbourhood were held in the fine Assembly Room.

An old bill of 1766 is preserved at the *Sun*. It was made out in William Marshall's time, and begins:

| To 11 Ordinaries | £0 | 16 | 6 |
| Wine | 0 | 9 | 0 |
| Punch | 0 | 3 | 0 |
| Men eating and beer | 0 | 2 | 6 |
| Tea | 0 | 3 | 0 |
| Suppers | 0 | 4 | 0 |

and after various other items concludes: " Mr. Freeman's Horse 1/8, Mr. Willis's Horse 4*d*." The total was £2 8*s*. 6*d*. of which only £1 8*s*. 6*d*. was paid. But it seems to have been a good feast, and a cheap one.

You should not leave the *Sun* without wandering through its big gardens, and seeing the old malt and brew houses, alas! no longer in use, reminders of the days when the inn brewed its own beer. Then you will realise how vast were the resources of a big coaching house.

From Hitchin turn back towards London and stop, after an eight-mile journey at the *George and Dragon* at Codicote. Opposite, two cross-roads, one from Luton, the other from St. Albans, join the Leeds turnpike, a guarantee that in the old days the *George and Dragon* was always busy.

It is a charming, gabled little house of brick and timber, with an overhanging upper storey built in the last years of Queen Elizabeth's reign. Like most old inns it has been altered a lot in its time. In the latter part of the eighteenth century its timbered front was rebuilt to the first floor and faced with roughcast above. In 1950 that roughcast was stripped off and the original half-timbering, some of it very good of its kind, revealed. The frames of two door-ways now out of use have been left undisturbed. The room to the right was the inn kitchen, and before its big open fireplace that now heats the Lounge, joints were roasted on a spit. There are old oak beams in nearly every room in the house, and its two brick chimney stacks with clustered shafts are unusual and worthy of notice.

Mr. Hine, who wrote of the *Sun* at Hitchin, believed that there was a *George and Dragon* standing here in Edward III.'s days when the inn belonged to St. Alban's Abbey and had to contribute its share of the fifty fowls and one pig each **Christmas and a thousand**

*The* George and Dragon, *an Elizabethan inn at Codicote.* (*Below*) *The sign of the* King's Arms, *Berkhamsted.* *The arms are, in fact, those of Queen Anne.*

(See Chapter 4)

*An old custom in Rye.  The Mayor throwing hot pennies to the children from the balcony of the* George.

(See Chapter 5)

*The porch of the* Rose & Crown *at Tonbridge, from the top of which the Master of the Skinners' Company used to acknowledge the greetings of the boys of Tonbridge School.*

(See Chapter 5)

*The* Dorset Arms *at Hartfield, a typical Sussex village inn close by Ashdown Forest.*

(See Chapter 5)

eggs and one pig each Easter which the village of Codicote paid to the Abbot.

Codicote was a busier place in old times, with a yearly Statute Fair and a weekly market held opposite the *George*, and at the inn much of the market and parish business was done. The church-wardens would adjourn to it to discuss their affairs. The manor court met there, and the tenants of Codicote Manor were entertained at an annual Rent Dinner after the meeting of the court. Straw plait made in the neighbourhood was sold in its courtyard and Mr. Hine tells of a tale of a dead and gone landlord, William Blain, whose custom it was regularly to read extracts from *The Times* to his "Parlour" customers for their instruction and edification.

Viewed from the front you might think that the gabled house adjoining was once part of the *George and Dragon*, but in fact a space of about two feet divides the houses, both much of an age, yet obviously never one. It is curious that the inn was not larger for it did quite a brisk trade in the posting days and boasted a dozen horses "at call" in its stables. But it is a very happy survival of the small posting inn and one must be immensely thankful it escaped a nineteenth-century rebuilding.

Another attractive example of the smaller inn is the *Cock* at Harpenden, a cross-country journey of about seven miles from Codicote. The *Cock*, or the *Old Cock* as they call it now, is a cheery, friendly sort of place, the favoured house of the better class shop-keepers of the village in past days. Here in 1818 they started a "Friendly Society of Tradesmen," a copy of the rules of which is preserved in the house. Those rules imposed a very strict standard of behaviour; members were forbidden to take tobacco within the club hours on pain of a fine of sixpence.

The *Old Cock's* extensive stables suggest a posting trade, but it was never a posting house. The stables were mostly used on Sundays by the good church people of the neighbourhood who drove in to attend service at Harpenden's fine parish church just behind the inn. There is nothing much older than the later eighteenth century in the fabric of the *Cock*, though probably there was a village inn here many centuries earlier. The oldest part is that facing the main road, now occupied by bars and Lounge.

From Harpenden make your way cross-country again for about twelve miles to Berkhamsted. It is a pretty drive through Hertford-shire by-ways, crossing the Great Holyhead Road at Redbourn, a very busy village in the Coaching Age, and at the *King's Arms*, Berkhamsted, you find one of the great posting inns of the old Birmingham road. Oddly enough the heraldic sign the *King's Arms* displays on its brick front is a queen's arms, that form of the Royal Arms used by Queen Anne between 1707 and 1714. Probably it was about this time that they rebuilt the old inn, erected its present pleasing red and black chequered brick front and hung out a new sign of a new sovereign's arms. The inn was twice its size then, comprising the whole of the adjoining building, to the right of the archway, as far as the corner.

Of the earlier inn there is not much more left than some old oak timbers and some brickwork in the cellars. The open hearth that you see as you enter the Lounge is old. It was discovered bricked up, during recent alterations. The attractive staircase that runs from the Lounge dates from the rebuilding. But happily many of the *King's Arms* old tales have survived. Berkhamsted's "Buttfield" where bowmen practised four or five hundred years ago was situated where the inn's garden is now. Writing in the middle of the last century, Cobb, in his history of Berkhamsted, said that he could distinctly trace "the position of the butt and where the archers stood to shoot."

Another old writer tells of the *King's Arms* in the posting days when horses and postilions were always in readiness in the inn yard. "The vehicles most in use," he says, "were the yellow post-chaises drawn by two and sometimes four horses." The postilions were dressed in gay coloured jackets and white hats, and the inn had an old retainer at that time, Abraham Bunn, who, though totally blind, acted as messenger, porter and guide, and is said never to have led any one astray though he conducted strangers to every part of the town and even to the neighbouring seats.

In the early years of the last century Louis XVIII., King of France, was a frequent patron of the *King's Arms*. He was living then in exile at Hartwell House near Aylesbury, and he habitually stopped at the inn to change horses when travelling to and from

London. Between the King and Mary Page, daughter of the landlord at that time, a real friendship grew up. Mary Page had the reputation of being a wonderful hostess, and when King Louis was restored to his throne he invited her to Paris, entertained her at the Royal Palace and sent her back to Berkhamsted with "many valuable souvenirs of the event which were treasured with much care as family relics," as it is recorded by Henry Nash, a writer who remembered her and her father John Page who died in 1840 at the age of 92.

Queen Victoria and the Prince Consort stopped to change horses at the *King's Arms* on their way to Woburn in 1841. The principal townsmen gathered on a platform erected in front of the inn to present a Loyal Address to the young queen and her husband, but the celebration was marred by the sudden death of Miss Sarah Page, sister of the proprietress, during the ceremony.

These are but some of the tales the *King's Arms* has to tell. You will find others in the records of the town and an untold one is the queer little landing between two of the, now, big front bedrooms. It was approached at one time by a narrow stair from the ground floor. Tradition says King Louis was accommodated here on his visits to the inn. Tradition may or may not be right, but tradition often is. These two rooms would have provided just the sort of private suite so distinguished a patron would have desired in which to rest and refresh while they changed the horses in his carriage, and old John Page and his daughter Mary entertained him before he took the road again ten miles on to his exile home at Hartwell, or eleven and a half miles towards London to Watford, where his next change of horses would have been made.

At Berkhamsted you have a choice of routes. You may follow the Birmingham road on through Aylesbury to the *White Hart* at Buckingham; make your way cross-country to the *Bedford Arms* at Woburn or the *Red Lion* at Luton, or, heading back towards London, turn right at King's Langley, a short six miles on your way, and stop at the *Two Brewers* at Chipperfield.

The *Two Brewers* was never anything more than a modest village inn and until recent years occupied only the middle one of the three houses it now comprises. But it is curiously attractive, looking over Chipperfield's wide common, with some oldish timber work and a pleasant yard at the back. In the last century it acquired a certain fame as training quarters for many of the great prize-fighters of the time, Jem Mace, Bob Fitzsimmons and Tom Sayers among them, trained here, sparred in the Club Room overlooking the yard, and took their runs round the common. Sometimes the local lads would spar with the champions and people drove from miles around to see the pugilists at work.

What is now the Lounge was formerly a stone-floored Tap Room with high-backed settles about the open fireplace, and as one of the *Two Brewers'* oldest customers says, regretfully: "Beer flowed free in those days." The old open fireplace is still there, modernised a little, and it is a pleasant place in front of which to sit over a tankard of ale and ponder those old days and the "sporting coves" who had come to see the champions, and their gigs that filled the inn yard, before you start on your 20-mile run back to London.

# CHAPTER FIVE

## South-East into Kent and Sussex

THIS IS going to be a rambling chapter, for our Kent and Sussex inns will not group themselves nicely together. So let us start, as the Pickwickians did, down the Dover road as far as Rochester, stopping at an inn along the High Street with a deplorable exterior and the sign of the *King's Head*.

How unprepossessing past owners of the *King's Head* have made its front is hard to express, but the house is a good example of what should be an axiom of lovers of old inns, never to trust to external appearances. There is an even better example in the *Red Lion* at Luton, but you will come to that later on. At the moment you stand depressed before what seems to be the most ordinary of provincial town pubs, then you go in and a pace or two takes you into the early eighteenth century, with survivals of the seventeeth and the sixteenth jostling it. Also it may be that you are entering the "Winglebury Arms" described by Charles Dickens in *Sketches by Boz*. For some say that the original of that was the *King's Head*.

There has been a house of entertainment on this spot since the year 1490, and Charles II. once spent a night here, so local historians record. In coaching days it was one of the principal posting houses of the city, and only a few yards separate it from the old College Gate, known to Dickens lovers as "Jasper's Gate House" in *Edwin Drood*.

To get a sense of the age of the inn it should be viewed from the back. There the steep-pitched roofs that cover the older part give a satisfying lie to its public-house front. They help to explain the Tudor beams and Jacobean panelling inside the inn. But the *King's Head's* two most notable features are its graceful Georgian staircase and the painted wall decoration on the first-floor landing. The mural painting, dark with age, is of classical subjects, not easily identified. There are little temples set on hills and a running stream and cascade as background to the figure groups. Painted pilasters divide the subjects, and such decoration tells of the importance of the *King's Head* when it was carried out in Queen Anne's time, or even earlier. In no ordinary inn would such work have been employed, and Rochester was ever a city of important inns.

On the upper floors there is a good deal of eighteenth-century panelling left—even a bathroom is panelled—and, cut up into small bedrooms, the old " Long Room " can be traced, at the front. From the back and side windows there are charming views of the adjacent Cathedral and " Jasper's Gate House." At the rear of the inn for years Rochester's Apple Market was held.

In traditions Rochester is as rich as any city in the country, and along the road in front of the *King's Head* the cavalcade of English history has passed from its beginning, for the High Street is part of the Watling Street of the Romans. In Rochester Museum is a section of its Roman cobbled paving, worn with deep ruts made by wheels that used the road close on two thousand years ago. By that very, very old road we leave Rochester and journey eastward for ten miles, then bear to the left into the marsh country, cross the river Swayle, and make for Sheerness.

Here in the Blue Town is the *Royal Fountain*, a Georgian inn the name of which is known the world over. For the *Fountain* is one of the British Navy's pet inns, right by Sheerness Dockyard and opposite the pier and the original landing hard of the town. Until the middle of the last century it was here that visitors to Sheerness arrived, for there was no bridge, and the *Fountain* welcomed them as they stepped ashore.

It is a jolly, breezy, hospitable old place and you will always find the Navy represented there. Indeed in other days it was not unusual for a ship's band to play in front of the *Fountain* when the officers were dining there, for all the world as though they were in their own mess. There must have been an inn here since Sheerness was first fortified in Charles II.'s reign, but the present house would have replaced it at the time of the Napoleonic Wars when the Dock-yard was enlarged. Old books tell of the rapid growth of the town at that time and of the erection of " a spacious hotel fitted up in a very superior style." That hotel was the *Fountain*.

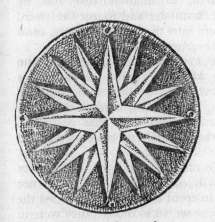

*When rooms were known by names and not by numbers: Door labels, at the Royal Fountain, Sheerness, of the " Rose," the " Crown," the " Star," and the " Sun " Rooms. The designs are in gilt on a grey-green background. The " Crown " label was stolen during the 1939/45 war.*

Its great feature is the first-floor corridor. Here is a very rare survival of the past. Four of the rooms retain the original signs of the names by which they were known in the days before guest chambers were merely numbered. There are the Sun, the Crown, the Rose and the Star rooms, each with its appropriate sign painted or japanned in heraldic style upon a metal disc. The doors themselves are pine-panelled with moulded frames, decorated at the top corners with little carved lion masks. This same lion decoration appears on the chimney-piece of a room leading from the pleasant bow-windowed Drawing-room, which was obviously used at one time as an Assembly Room.

From many of the second floor windows fine views of the Medway may be seen. The walls of the corridor, and some of the bedrooms on this floor, have behind their wallpapers a simple decorative design apparently stencilled on to the plaster, now grown hard as stone. One of the more attractive rooms in the house is the Smoking-room leading off the Entrance Hall, an intimate little chamber with simple painted wainscoting running half-way up the walls. You feel that in this room first-hand tales of the British Navy since the days of Nelson have been told.

Sheerness and the Isle of Sheppey are not well known to the average tourist, and a detour to Minster's Abbey Church three miles away and a visit to Queenborough, on the way back to the mainland, are worth the making. Queenborough was founded by Edward III. and takes its name from his queen, Philippa.

Our next few inns are scattered and fall in with no regular itinerary, some inland, some farther to the east, and you must choose for yourself how you will take them. But the Dickens lover should go east to the *Royal Albion* at Broadstairs for this is a true Dickens inn, not in the usually accepted sense but an inn which he loved, at which he stayed for long periods and in which he worked.

The *Albion* is described as "a new-built house conveniently fitted up," in a Guide of 1816. Mr. Peyton, formerly of the older *Rose* inn, was the first landlord. That original *Albion* would have been the present corner block. But it soon enlarged itself and eventually absorbed a lodging house, now part of the other end of the

*One of the oldest inns in Sussex.  The* Star *at Alfriston, built for a pilgrim's hostel in the fifteenth century.*

(See Chapter 5)

*A good example of a "gallows" signpost at the* George, Crawley.
(See Chapter 5)

*The White Horse at Dorking, which has mysterious cellars and a pedigree going back to the Knights Templars.*

(See Chapter 5)

*The* Dolphin *at Southampton. Its bow windows are believed to be the biggest of their kind in existence.*

(See Chapter 6)

hotel, where in 1839 Charles Dickens was staying when he finised *Nicholas Nickleby*. Writing to a friend of his life at Broadstairs a couple of years later, he told of an innkeeper to whom his frequent demands for ale and cold punch must have given great satisfaction. That innkeeper was probably landlord of the *Albion*, next door to Dickens's lodgings, for the *Albion* was famed for its milk punch in the early 'forties.

In 1845 Dickens and his family spent August at the *Albion*. He was back again in 1847 and wrote of looking from his window, "out upon a dark grey sea with a keen north-east wind blowing it on shore." It was while staying at the *Albion* in 1849, that he wrote Chapter XI of *David Copperfield*. His last visit to the hotel was in 1859. By then, as he said, the town had grown "too noisy" to please him. One of his autographed letters hangs on the wall of the Lounge. Written in 1841 it tells his appreciation of Broadstairs' "good sea, fresh breezes, fine sands . . . and all manner of fishing boats, lighthouses, piers, bathing machines and so forth."

The *Albion* has retained many of the features it possessed when Dickens stayed there, though curiously there are no traditional "Dickens Rooms." He probably used too many. But the Hotel Bar now comprises the two ground floor rooms, the "best rooms" of the lodging-house in which he stayed in 1839, and it is not a wild surmise to think that it was in the back room overlooking the sea that he wrote the last chapters of *Nicholas Nickleby*.

The ancient Cinque Port of Sandwich is only nine miles from Broadstairs, and as you enter the town, across the bridge the *Bell Inn* faces you as it faced King Charles II. when he rode in with the Duke of York and Prince Rupert in 1669. On that occasion, the annals of the town record, the king was met by the mayor who: "presented His Majesty with a glass of sack at the *Bell* tavern door, which His Majesty drank on horseback."

That *Bell* tavern has given place to a modern building although not all so modern as it appears. There are Georgian survivals. The present Dining-room was the Assembly Room of posting days. It is a handsome room with a Musicians' Gallery and an elaborately decorated doorway painted in black and gold, adorned with ball and lion mask decoration. There is an old-fashioned bar of the same

*John Revell's half penny trade token issued at the* Bell Inn, *Sandwich, in the mid-seventeenth century.*

period, but for the rest, there is little of the building more than forty years old, and perhaps the only relic of the *Bell* that Charles II. saw is a token issued by John Revell, landlord about the time when the King stopped there, a specimen of which is displayed in the house.

Another Cinque Port inn of interest is the *George* at Rye. This is one of the older inns of that ancient town, but there is a streak of mystery in its story. In the early seventeen hundreds, it moved from what is known as the " Butchery," opposite the present Town Hall, to the house it has occupied ever since, at the corner of High Street and Lion Street. Why this move was made is not known. The old house in which it carried on business for so long still stands, and the house to which it moved is perhaps as old, a timber building of Tudor date. This house must have been standing for nearly two centuries when the *George* moved its sign and trade to it in the days of Queen Anne or the early years of George I.'s reign.

Lion Street, by the way, takes its name from the old *Red Lyon* inn, which was burnt down in 1872. Its site is now occupied by a school. It stood within a stone's throw of the original *George* and the two inns are connected in one of the old tales of that inn. This occurred in 1687 when Moses Peadle, of a well-known and respected Rye family, was imprisoned in the Freeman's Hall close by " for swearing nine oaths." Moses Peadle made a habit of escaping from his custody by night to go drinking at the *George* and the *Red Lyon*. And for his drunkenness, he was disenfranchised by the outraged borough authorities.

After its move, the *George* certainly became the "Head Inn" of the town—not only were all the great municipal functions held there, but in due course it became the principal posting and coaching inn of Rye. It has seen many changes—as have all such old inns— and has undergone periodic improvements and alterations. In the *George* to-day you may see examples of the taste and craftsmanship of fully four hundred years.

Externally, the house was modernised in the middle seventeen hundreds, probably about 1760. There is a leaden fire mark of the Sun Insurance Office fixed to the wall over the door which leads to the little balcony above the main entrance. The number on this fire mark dates it as having been issued by the Company in about that year. The ironwork of the railings of this balcony, the design of the door and also the design of the main door beneath, all belong to about the same period. Inside the *George* much of the original construction can be seen in the richly raftered ceilings and oakbeamed walls.

But though there is much of earlier workmanship, the character and atmosphere of the inn to-day is that of the hospitable Georgian Coaching and Posting House, and its pride is its really fine Ballroom, dating from the later years of George III.'s reign.

Yet, before the *George's* fine Ballroom was built, there are records of entertainment at the inn. In the eighteenth century, Rye's Annual Herring Feast was held each year, alternately at the *George* and the *Red Lyon*. The Barons of the Cinque Ports were entertained at the *George* from time to time, and a distinguished guest was the Duke of Wellington, when Lord Warden of the Cinque Ports.

The little balcony of the old Long Room must have many tales to tell also. From it the results of Rye's heated elections were announced. Whig and Liberal candidates addressed excited crowds from it, for the *George* was the Whig house of Rye. And newly-elected members returned thanks from it. Each year the newly-chosen Mayor appeared on the balcony and carried out one of Rye's ancient customs, that of throwing hot pennies to the children in the street beneath. This custom, which was abandoned in the first black days of the war, was revived in 1944.

As a coaching and posting inn, the *George* was the most important house in Rye. Some of its old stabling may still be seen in the yard behind, and the main coach entrance was under an arch below the Ballroom. The way out was into Lion Street by the gates that still remain. A regular coach service to London was started in 1778 with the "Diligence," a lumbering affair that took 16 hours to do the 63 mile journey, travelling up one day and down the next. By 1812, the time had been reduced to 13 hours, and there was a thrice-weekly service between the *George* and the *Bolt-in-Tun*, Fleet Street, London. Fourteen years later, a daily coach was running between the same two inns in 9 hours, and a year or so later still, the Hastings-Margate coach was calling twice daily at the *George*.

To another *George*—the *George* at Cranbrook in the Weald of Kent—we now make our way. The route takes us along the old coach road across the "Isle" of Oxney, which is the western fringe of Romney Marsh. The *George* at Cranbrook is an interesting old inn with tales of Queen Elizabeth and French prisoners to tell.

It is an ancient, red-roofed house, with tile-hung front, now little more than half its former size, rich in moulded beams and open fireplaces. But its pride is a magnificent oak staircase, with heavy balusters, that sweeps from the entrance hall to the first-floor landing. It has been in place for well over 200 years and was probably an improvement of some landlord in William and Mary's reign.

Cranbrook was a prosperous cloth-weaving town and when Queen Elizabeth visited it local history tells that she stopped at the *George* and was presented with a silver cup by the town's rich clothiers. Tradition assigns an upstairs chamber as the room in which she received her loyal subjects. The room appears to have been an ante-room to the adjacent Great Court Room, now divided into smaller rooms, and suggests that the queen used it as a retiring chamber, and received the clothiers in the larger room. After the ceremony, it is told, the queen walked a mile from the *George* to Coursehorn Manor on a carpet of the town's famous grey broadcloth which the clothiers had caused specially to be woven for the purpose.

The French prisoner tale is a curious one and must have some connection with the Tudor mansion of Sissinghurst, a couple of miles away, which housed French prisoners during the Seven Years' War of the middle-eighteenth century. According to long-standing tradition in Cranbrook, certain strange black marks, suggesting initials and dates, discovered on a corridor ceiling on the top floor some years ago, were made by French prisoners incarcerated at the *George*. The marks are whitewashed over now but the date 1760 was discernible among them. Further, at the end of the corridor are remains of irons attached to a strong cross-beam in the floor to which, so the story goes, the prisoners were chained. Perhaps the explanation is that for very many years the local Magistrates sat in the Great Court Room and before them recalcitrant French prisoners as well as local offenders were brought, and this upstairs corridor was used as a temporary cell for both.

The inn's present Dining-room was once the kitchen and retains its open hearth with an oak chimney-beam of ten feet in span. There is a good specimen of the old "Coaching" or "Act of Parliament" clock hanging in the entrance hall, the work of a local maker, and much nice old furniture about the house.

From Cranbrook, through typical, homely, Kentish scenery, marked by oast houses and hop fields, the road leads nineteen miles on to the *Rose and Crown* at Tonbridge, one of the great posting inns of the old Winchelsea and Hastings road. Its pleasing front of chequered blue and red brick is of the earlier 1700's. Inside, old beams and stretches of Jacobean panelling tell of a house fully a hundred years older.

To the *Rose and Crown* once a year, in July, come the Master, Wardens and Court of the Skinner's Company on their annual visit to Tonbridge School, founded by Sir Andrew Judd, a native of the town, and a member of the Skinner's Company in Edward VI.'s reign. Room seventeen is the Master's room on these occasions. Its windows give access to the top of the entrance porch from which the Master acknowledged the greetings of the Tonbridge boys, who, by old custom, assembled outside the inn early in the morning of the last Saturday in July, to give their Governors a hearty welcome. Some old labels inscribed with the names of the principal officers of the Company, formerly hung upon the doors of the rooms they occupied, are preserved at the inn.

The *Rose and Crown* had many distinguished visitors in the posting days. Queen Victoria as a girl was here, and the arms of her parents the Duke and Duchess of Kent are displayed over the porch. The inn had some years ago a well-known and popular landlord in the old Kent cricketer, Tom Pawley.

Journeying on, past Tunbridge Wells, where, at the modern *Wellington Hotel*, there is an extraordinary collection of prints and relics of the Great Duke of Wellington, including the dispatch case he used at Waterloo, the road by the Medway valley leads to two attractive little tile-hung inns on the fringe of Ashdown Forest. Both bear the same sign, the *Dorset Arms*, and the first of them, at Withyham, stands almost at the gates of Buckhurst Park, the ancient seat of the Sackvilles, sometime Earls of Dorset.

The *Dorset Arms* at Withyham was known as Somers farmhouse in Queen Elizabeth's days, but it had become an inn in the eighteenth century, when it is marked on a map simply as " The Ale House." A very modest wayside inn it must have been for the road past it is described in the Road Books of 1810 as: " Bad for carriages and in winter impassable." But it had its trade with those who came and went to Buckhurst, and twice a year when Withyham held its cattle and pedlary fairs. It has not been spoiled, rather it has been improved in recent years by the removal of matchboard partitions and wallpapers and plaster that hid its old oak beams. It numbers among its features a Tudor fireplace, some carved stone mullions and transoms to a blocked-up window on the ground floor, and a simple eighteenth-century staircase.

Its namesake at Hartfield, a mile and a half farther on, is of the same period, but more of a village than a wayside inn. It too is full of oak, and has, at the back, now used as a storeroom, its ancient kitchen with open hearths and bread ovens in the wall, the old crane for suspending pots and kettles and a good Sussex iron fire-back. The Hartfield *Dorset Arms* has preserved much of its old equipment, Georgian decanters, cordial bottles that once

*An Abbot or Bishop, probably St. Giles, fifteenth-century carving on the front of the* Star, *Alfriston.*

decorated the Bar, and one of those cone-shaped ale warmers found less and less frequently in inns now, the utensil in which our forefathers heated their drink of a winter's night by the simple process of placing the ale warmer in the embers of the hearth.

There is interesting country close by Withyham and Hartfield. Ashdown Forest rises to just 800 feet at Crowborough Beacon three miles distant, and The Rocks or Penn's Rocks a mile and a half from Withyham was a house of William Penn's family.

Hartfield is perhaps the best place on this route from which to make excursion to one of the most important of old Sussex inns, the *Star* at Alfriston. It entails a trip of nearly thirty miles, but it takes you at the beginning clean across Ashdown Forest, then through the Sussex Weald to the South Downs. There in a narrow valley through which the little river Cuckmere winds to the sea is ancient Alfriston and the *Star*, the origin of which is in "the mist of antiquity" one old writer asserts.

Less picturesque writers claim an early fifteenth-century origin. With that modern antiquaries agree, though one of them goes further and calls it "perhaps the oldest inn in Sussex." But as to who founded it they still argue. It is undoubtedly ecclesiastical in origin and it is generally accepted now to have been built by the great Abbey of Battle, and that its sign is that of the Star of Bethlehem.

It was probably a pilgrim's inn, offering shelter to the faithful making their way to the shrine of St. Richard at Chichester. To call it picturesque is trite: the house has unique features. Its roof is of half-hundredweight slabs of colourful Horsham stone. The timbers of its front are elaborately and skilfully carved in a variety of subjects. But with them the idol-like lion at the corner must not be confused. He was the figurehead of a ship wrecked on the neighbouring coast some three hundred years ago. The *Star's* really old carvings are on the timbers of the building itself: the lion and monkey on a corner post, St. Michael and the basilisk, the two snakes and the shield below the oriel windows, the quaint little faces seen here and there, the terrier dog and the mitred figure of an abbot or bishop, probably St. Giles, all of which adorn the front of the inn.

The massive oak front-door is old, but of Tudor date like the open hearths in some of the rooms. There is a roasting jack still in place over the open fireplace in the Lounge, implying that this was once the inn kitchen. Oak studs or wall timbers, and oak rafters are in practically every room of the old part of the house and there is a sense of immense age about the *Star*. This is a house that was being built about the time of the Battle of Agincourt, and in one way is even more interesting than the *Red Lion* of Colchester or the *Blue Boar* at Maldon, with both of which it may be compared, because it was built to be an inn and it has continued to be an inn throughout five hundred years of England's history.

The antiquity of the place incites superlatives. You cannot describe it otherwise nor Alfriston itself, a village of ancient buildings of which the *Star* is but one, though maybe as old as any. E. V. Lucas called it "the best of primitive villages." Arthur Beckett, a local writer, "the dreamplace of the downland explorer." Let it go at that. You will count your thirty-mile run from Hartfield a well-spent effort when you have seen Alfriston and its *Star* and come, a little blasé perhaps, to the *George* at Crawley, though that be a very old inn. But it has a Regency atmosphere to leaven its ancient timbers and tales to tell of Corinthian Bucks driving hell for leather down the road to Brighton to provide a contrast to the pious pilgrims who first used the *Star*.

You come to Crawley from Alfriston as your mood and your map takes you. From Hartfield the way is by East Grinstead and Three Bridges, a journey of about sixteen miles, passing close by Crawley Downs and Copthorne Common, scenes of many historic prize fights in Regency days.

In *Rodney Stone*, Conan Doyle drew a vivid picture of the extra-

*A good example of the interior of what was once an open gallery, later covered for the greater comfort of travellers. This gallery is at the* White Horse, *Romsey.*

(See Chapter 6)

*The portico of the* White Hart *at Salisbury. The sign was erected in 1820 to challenge that of a nearby rival.*

(See Chapter 6)

*The* Lansdowne Arms, *formerly the Catherine Wheel, at Calne. A typical posting house on the Bath Road.*

(See Chapter 6)

*The skittle alley in the old wing of the* Methuen Arms *at Corsham.*
(See Chapter 6)

ordinary scenes these fights provided. They were attended by thousands of all classes from the Prince Regent himself downwards, every road leading towards the scene of the fight being as thick with traffic as the roads to Epsom on Derby Day. Conan Doyle made the *George* the inn at which Belcher trained Boy Jim for his fight with Crab Wilson.

Of the house's earliest days there is no record save in the four and five-hundred-year-old work in its fabric. And that tells of a building of importance. A carved King Post is hidden by the ceiling of one of the

*Grotesque human face carved on a beam at the* Star, *Alfriston.*

bedrooms, a part of the roof of what was probably a mediæval Hall. There is a very early window to be seen from the staircase, long since blocked up, that once looked out upon the garden. It is a primitive little thing, with simple mullions and it was never glazed, being closed only by crude shutters. The stone fireplace in the entrance hall is said to have been brought from another house. It is with little doubt some years older than 1615, the date inscribed upon it. And probably because of that date the *George*, according to local tradition, became an inn in that year.

The tradition may be truth, but the inn would not have done much trade until after 1696 when a causeway for horsemen was constructed from Reigate to Crawley. That causeway was widened sixty years later and the Brighton road, as we know it, came into being. Thence onward the *George* flourished. Its rare gallows sign-post stretching across the highway became a feature of the road. Rowlandson drew it in 1789 showing a picturesque front to the inn that must have been altered only a few years later when the Regent had made Brighton the fashion and coaches, gigs and chaises streamed along the road and most of them stopped at the half-way house, the *George*. At the end of the Posting Era, its business was enormous. London coaches called there hourly in

T.O.I.                                                                                    F

1839. Then the railways came and the *George* went into eclipse, to revive with the coming of the motor car, when again it became the custom of "everybody" to stop at the old inn.

At Crawley again a choice of routes presents itself. If your road be back to London, strike across country, or turn left at Reigate and see the *White Horse* at Dorking on the way.

For some reason the *White Horse* has acquired the tradition of being the original "Marquis of Granby" of *Pickwick Papers*. It cannot have been, for Mr. Weller's "Markis," as readers of *Pickwick* know, was a much more humble inn. The *White Horse* when Sam Weller travelled to Dorking was the great posting house of the town. It is a very old place, known formerly as the "Cross House," from the Maltese Cross badge of its one time owners the Knights of St. John of Jerusalem. Before their time, the Knights Templars had a building on its site which passed to the Knights of St. John in 1278.

It is an attractive rambling house, most of it fully four centuries old, and there are the traditions of mysterious underground passages beneath it that so often cling to very old buildings. Certainly its cellars are old and interesting. They are cut in sandstone and from them a curious passage of well-worn steps descends to end in the shaft of an ancient well. Its walls are covered with carved names and initials and dates, many of them of the early years of the eighteenth century. The head of the well is covered by a slab in the courtyard. Were that well ever cleared out there would be some interesting finds to be made.

The *White Horse* claims to have in its pleasant garden the biggest apple tree in the South of England. It is of great age, yet still yields an average of about twenty-eight bushels of "Lord Derbys" each season.

The alternative route from Crawley is westward by way of Horsham to the Chichester road. At Horsham the *Black Horse*, though a mid-Victorian building, is on the site of a much earlier inn. There is record of a *Black Horse Inn* in West Street in 1690. The present inn, of course, developed with the Worthing Road, which was constructed in 1764. The inn prospered and by 1841 had become one of the town's most important houses, the headquarters of the

"Pinks," an independent Tory party of the time. The "Pinks" held champagne suppers here in 1847, and it would have been rebuilt soon afterwards. It now embraces a Corn Exchange built in 1866, and where corn dealers once set up their desks on Market days is the Dining-room of the present inn.

At Chichester, about twenty-five miles on, facing the cathedral and close by the old Market Cross, is the *Dolphin and Anchor*, two rival inns now united under the dual sign.

The *Dolphin* was always the more important. An eighty-year-old guide-book described it well as, "Excellent and not without a certain gravity befitting an episcopal city." But it endured a lot from its rival the *Anchor*. The *Dolphin* was the Whig inn, while the *Anchor* was the Tory house, and the rivalry of the *Anchor* inspired an advertisement in the London *Star* of 7th July, 1792, from Mr. J. Parsons who had recently taken over the *Dolphin*. He said:

"Gentlemen and Ladies travelling in Post Chaises are particularly desired to order Postillions to drive to the *Dolphin*, as various Arts are used to prevent the good intentions of J. Parsons' friends."

The inn has an attractive yard, with a picturesque range of old buildings along one side, approached through an archway where the meat and game hooks still remain. It had famous landlords in its time, men important in their city's affairs. The widow of one of them, James Ballard, whose Warrant of Posting Master to Queen Victoria hangs in the inn's main hall, died in 1874 and is still remembered as the last person to use a sedan chair in Chichester. When the *Dolphin* first opened its doors is unknown, but a stone dated 1519 found built into an old chimney gives a clue, and behind the Georgian and early Victorian decoration of the inn of to-day there must be much of the old fabric hidden.

Westward the great Bristol to Margate cross-road of posting days, and the highway from Regnum, which was Chichester, to Porchester, the Roman Portus Magnus, leads in a few miles into Hampshire.

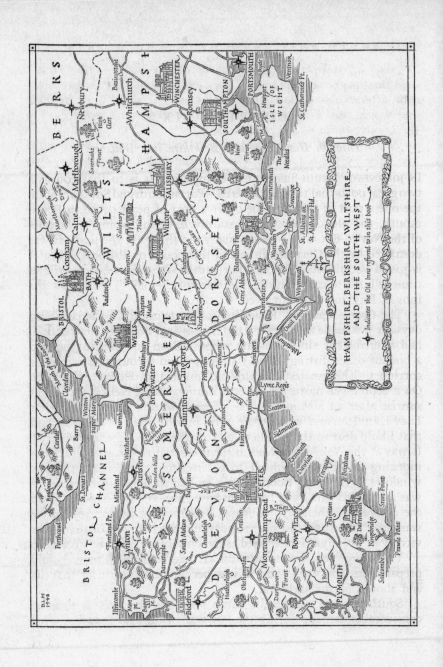

HAMPSHIRE, BERKSHIRE, WILTSHIRE, AND THE SOUTH WEST

✶ Indicates the Old Inns referred to in this book

# CHAPTER SIX

### *Through Hampshire and Berkshire into Wiltshire*

IN JOURNEYING from Sussex into Hampshire, it is to that county's two great ports that the road leads us—Portsmouth and Southampton, the one a port of war and the other a port of peace. And in Portsmouth, the old *George* could certainly have told some great tales of the Navy. But alas!—like so many old things of the past—it was destroyed by the Germans in one of their raids on the port. Now it is just a vacant site. But on that vacant site a new *George* will in time be built to carry on the traditions of the old. That is how the inns of England have survived.

The *George* was the "Head Inn" of Portsmouth in the coaching days. It was made up of several old houses and, before its destruction, had altered little since the days when Nelson and Wellington and a host of other distinguished visitors walked through its rambling corridors. The greatest tale this old inn had to tell was of Nelson. On a September morning in 1805, Admiral Lord Nelson arrived at sunrise after an all-night journey from Merton where he had left Lady Hamilton and, as he wrote in his private diary on the way, "all that I hold dear in this world to go to serve my King and Country." It was at the *George* that Nelson spent his last hours ashore. In the morning he showed himself to a cheering crowd from the bay windows of the Long Room. After he had spoken to the people, he was smuggled out by a back staircase into Penny Street to avoid the crowd and thence to Southsea beach where he embarked. He was never to return, but his memory and the memory of that great victory at Trafalgar is cherished as the symbol of our naval greatness.

The *George* was a warrior's inn. It had seen much of wars and preparations for wars—and it was perhaps not unfitting that its end should be through war.

Southampton, too, has its battle scars and the *Dolphin* suffered considerable damage during the last war in the raid that destroyed

85

much of the High Street. The *Dolphin* was old in 1620 when the Pilgrim Fathers set sail in the *Mayflower* from Southampton Quay. Here you will come upon stories of the immortal Jane Austen. She used regularly to attend the dances held in the *Dolphin's* big Assembly Room and in a letter wrote that she intended going to as many as possible that she might "have a good bargain" on her subscription. That was in 1808 when Jane, her sister Cassandra and her mother were staying in the town and the *Dolphin's* Winter Assemblies were highly fashionable functions, even attended by Royalty. The room in which Jane danced, now the Dining-room, is one of the best examples of the well-designed Assembly Rooms of the important inn in Georgian days. It has a commodious ante-chamber leading from it, where the Buffet would have been set out or whist tables arranged.

Later in the last century Thackeray stayed at the *Dolphin* and wrote part of *Pendennis* there. In earlier years it entertained Gibbon the historian, the King of Morocco, who was lavishly feasted by the Mayor and Corporation, Archbishop Laud's Commissaries sent to inquire, in 1635, into the backslidings of Southampton's church folk, and, in 1648, John Taylor the "Water Poet," who wrote of his journey that it took him three days from London, though as he recorded of the horses:

"And brought us to the *Dolphin* at Southampton.
With fiery speed and foaming bit they champt on."

For the *Dolphin* is a very old inn. There is mention of it in records of 1506 when its tenant was brought before the Mayor and ordered to repair the house on pain of "forfeiting his indentures of the same house." But it was drastically reconstructed in the middle-eighteenth century and only a few fragments of the Tudor inn have survived, small stretches of half-timber wall and two stone mullioned windows. In the main it is good middle Georgian, the modern inn of the early years of George III.'s reign, and a really fine old posting house. Its huge bow windows in the front are said to be the largest of their kind known, and within memory its meat and game hung in the archway and the visitor demanding a chop or a steak could see the cook, coming out from his kitchen in the yard, haul down a joint and cut it for him. In 1914 it was Haig's headquarters while the Expeditionary Force was embarking for France. And in this last war it suffered from blast in the raid which set much of the High Street ablaze. The damage was increased when the premises opposite were declared unsafe and blown up.

At the *White Horse* at Romsey, eight miles away, you come to an older inn and one that has not suffered much from change. It has the Georgian brick front that so many of these Tudor inns acquired, but inside it is a glorious place of rough old-timbered walls and ceilings, and on one of the wall beams of the Lounge a portion of a painted design, which probably originally, covered the whole wall, survives. The design includes a repetition of the Tudor dragon, and there is another stretch of wall painting in the Bar where a less delicate design on a big panel of plaster includes the Tudor rose.

Traditionally the house once belonged to Romsey's grand Norman Abbey close by. Perhaps it was a Guest House of the good nuns there. But it was obviously rebuilt or reconstructed in the early fifteen hundreds, maybe after the dissolution of the Monasteries, perhaps earlier. There are remains of an older structure in the cellars where part of a Gothic window and the entrance to a long-ago bricked up passage may be seen.

The inn is built about a narrow courtyard, and the galleries, from which the bedrooms lead, once open to the yard itself, are still there though closed against the weather. The *White Horse* is unusually rich in old furniture and there is a very human reminder of other days in the written announcement that hangs on one of the walls, and reads:

"This days Bill of Fare will contain Turbot and Fried Soles, Lobster sauce, Leg of Mutton, 6 Tooth wether, Swanston Lea Lamb and Sparagrass. Grass Fed Beef and all varieties to satisfy the Inner Man."

Could one ask a better meal?

The *White Hart* at Salisbury, sixteen miles farther on, is an inn of very definite character. An ancient house of many tales, it was completely rebuilt somewhere about 1800. Its imposing portico is its great feature. Surmounting it is a more than life-size *White Hart* gazing defiantly at the city. It was placed there in 1827 to outdo a new sign erected by a, then, rival inn, the *Antelope*, close by.

Some Dickens students identify the *White Hart* with that "very first hotel in the town" at which John Westlock gave his wonderful dinner to Tom Pinch and Martin Chuzzlewit. "A famous Inn!" Dickens described it, "the hall a very grove of dead game and dangling joints of mutton . . ."

It is a huge place, occupying nearly an acre. At the old house, which the present one replaced, Henry VII. is said to have stayed. Sir Walter Raleigh, in 1618, returned to England in disgrace, was in the city at the time that James I. was there, and was afraid to meet him. So he feigned sickness in his lodging, though it is recorded his French medical attendant: "procured from the *White Hart* inn a leg of mutton and some loaves which Raleigh devoured in secret and ·thus led his attendants to suppose that he took no kind of sustenance." Another unfortunate man associated with the *White Hart* was Henry Laurens, sometime President of the American Congress, who was taken prisoner by a British warship while on his way to Holland in 1780. He spent a night at the inn, in custody of a British Naval officer, on his way to London where he spent fourteen months in the Tower. His could not have been very pleasant memories of the old inn, though one hopes that the Naval officer lived up to the hospitable traditions of his service and did his best for his unhappy captive.

Salisbury is a convenient place from which to visit Wilton, four and a half miles away, not only to see a pleasant little inn, the *Pembroke Arms*, beneath which and through its garden a trout stream runs, which is at least unusual, but Wilton House, the magnificent mansion of the Earls of Pembroke, where among other treasures is a collection of Vandyck portraits displayed in the Double Cube room expressly designed for them by Inigo Jones. The house is open to the public at stated times and the *Pembroke Arms* stands close by its gates.

The original *Pembroke Arms* stood on the other side of the road.

*Moulded plaster overmantel at the* Luttrel Arms, *Dunster, probably fashioned by the same hand as a similar one in the Castle, dated* 1620.
(See Chapter 7)

*The " Kingsley Room" at the* Royal Hotel, *Bideford, constructed in
1688 for a Bideford Merchant Adventurer.*
(See Chapter 7)

*Porch of the* White Hart, *Moretonhampstead, Devon.* The
*sign, curiously, is that of a hind, not a hart.*
(See Chapter 7)

*Chambermaids' bells on a landing at the* Castle, *Windsor.*
(See Chapter 8)

The present house dates from the early years of the last century, and its sign, the silver lions of the Pembrokes, hangs from an unusual wrought-iron support, cleverly fashioned to show the raised spikes of an earl's coronet, that must have come from the older inn. You are in George Herbert's country here. Fugglestone church, a few hundred yards from the *Pembroke Arms*, is of the mother parish of Bemerton, nearer Salisbury, where the saintly poet-parson lived.

From Salisbury, too, you should visit the *White Hart* at Whitchurch, twenty-four miles up the London road. The *White Hart* was a famous junction inn in posting days. It stands at the corner where the east to west London-Exeter road crosses the north to south turnpike from Oxford to Southampton. And here the traveller of old days waited with commendable patience when he had to change coaches.

The *White Hart* was established traditionally in 1461. But all, save a few fragments, of that original house were destroyed in a reconstruction a couple of hundred years and more ago. But they put up a good new house in its place, and Charles Kingsley, who stayed at the inn in the 1860's, was impressed by one of its features. "I like the place and that is truth," he wrote in a letter. "It is old without being decayed. This low room has a beautiful Queen Anne's ceiling. . . . Oh dear ! I have had such a jolly day, and the lamb chops are so good, and there is such a sponge bath in my room . . ."

The "Queen Anne's ceiling" is that of the present Dining-room, and it is probably of earlier date.

Another parson-author was at the inn thirty years before, in 1832. He was the Rev. John Henry Newman, later Cardinal Newman, and while waiting from one to eleven o'clock for the down Exeter Mail, he composed the opening verses of his "Lyra Apostolica." Later he was to write some better known verses, those of the hymn, "Lead Kindly Light." Whitchurch is one of the many little towns that flourished exceedingly during the Coaching Age and languished at its death. It is a place of echoes of the heyday of the road, and at the *White Hart* one of the swiftest coaches in England stopped regularly, the "Telegraph" that did the 170 odd miles from London to Exeter in the amazing time of seventeen hours.

At Newbury, sixteen miles from the *White Hart*, you strike the

Bath Road. Speenhamland they call the part of the town through which that historic highway runs, and Speenhamland was noted for its posting inns. Of one of them, the *Pelican*, a wit wrote that it:

> "May well be called the Pelican
> From its enormous bill."

The *Chequers* inn here was a smaller posting house where the country stages called. The house was drastically altered in 1833, but parts of an older structure remain in the oak beams of the Bar, formerly the kitchen.

The *Castle and Ball* at Marlborough, twenty miles farther down the Bath road, is one of the few houses in Marlborough's wide High Street that escaped the devastating fires that twice swept through the town. It is a Tudor inn, full of oak, but its front was set back a few feet in later days, perhaps after one of the fires when they were rebuilding the street. The inn has seen fighting in its time, for through its courtyard Cavalier soldiers rushed in a surprise attack on the Parliamentarians during the Civil War.

Seen from the rear it is obvious that the house was originally much larger and included an adjoining building. It has been suggested that this was the *Hart* at which Samuel Pepys stayed when he visited Marlborough in 1668. That tale needs proof, but local historians place the *Hart* as close by if not adjoining, and say that the inns of the town changed their names with perplexing frequency.

The *Castle and Ball's* odd sign is also a matter of conjecture. It has used the name since the coaching days certainly. Possibly it is a corruption of *Castle and Bull*, two of the charges in the arms of Marlborough which figured on a town token of the mid-seventeenth century. So in the Pepys tradition and the origin of the sign are two yet untold tales for the lover of old inns to seek out.

The next stage down the Bath road, the post-boys of the late eighteenth century would have told you, was to the *Wheel* at Calne, the *Catherine Wheel*, an impressive spacious stone-tiled, flat-fronted old coaching and posting inn occupying most of one side of the Strand, Calne's market square. But the *Catherine Wheel* changed its name early in the nineteenth century and became the *Lansdowne Arms*, since then displaying the quarterings of the shield of the Marquis of Lansdowne whose country seat is just outside the town.

The tale of the *Lansdowne Arms* is that of so many of the great posting inns of the road. It began perhaps in the Middle Ages, it is mentioned frequently in the borough records of Queen Elizabeth's reign, and then in the middle of the eighteenth century, when the road was improved and rank and fashion driving to Bath abandoned the older way through Devizes and streamed through Calne instead, the old *Catherine Wheel* was enlarged by rebuilding and taking in adjoining houses. The oldest part of the house is to the extreme left when seen from the front. Here are stone mullioned windows and early oak. For the rest the *Lansdowne Arms* is typical of coach and post-chaise Georgian England.

The inn has fortunately preserved some relics of those days, many of them lain forgotten in disused stable buildings or attics for years. There is a post-boy's strapped leather bag among the relics, the steps that were put to the coach doors for the convenience of alighting passengers, and a cabinet of brightly polished bits. In the yard behind, the inn's old Brew House remains, and painted boldly on a wall there is the hospitable greeting: "Welcome ye coming Speed ye parting Guest."

There is another old inn that changed its sign ten miles farther on the way to Bath. Turn left about four miles beyond Chippenham and make a short detour by Corsham, and at the *Methuen Arms*, once the *Red Lion*, is perhaps a unique relic of an ancient inn custom. On the stone posts of the Public Bar entrance there survives the painted chequer design that was for centuries the almost universal indication, quite apart from the sign of the house itself, of a tavern or house of refreshment. In old pictures this chequered painting is often shown around the sign board's supporting post. Hogarth's picture "Beer Street" shows it in this position. In other examples it is, as at Corsham, on the door posts or the wall of the inn. Its origin some authorities claim is Roman, and a similar design has been found on inns in Pompeii. There has been much controversy about its meaning, and when Larwood, historian of Sign Boards, wrote in 1866, the custom was fast dying out. Recent letters of inquiry to the Press for other surviving examples of this sign have produced no result. Therefore maybe the *Methuen Arms* example is unique.

The inn itself is an interesting one, apart from its rare sign, that has developed from a mediæval house, known as Winter's Court, a seat of the Nott family from the fifteenth century. The Notts held it until 1732 and in their time it became an inn. There are Nott initials; "N.N. I.N. 1650" carved on the wall of the very old wing facing Laycock Road and beneath them: "C.W., 1749," are initials of Christine Webber, a descendant of the family. The dates would record alterations done in those years.

The front block of the inn is a Georgian building, at the back is a Tudor wing with stone arched fireplaces in two of the rooms. There is an ancient skittle alley in this wing, which was at one time the inn's Brew House and Malting, and at the end of the yard a picturesque barn, the top of its wall pierced for a dove cote.

This old house had become an inn by 1608; in 1637 there is record of it as the *Red Lion*, and that name it bore probably until the rebuilding, about 1805, when it changed its sign to the arms of the Methuen family of Corsham Hall nearby, into whose possession it had passed. There is a picture of the old house before the rebuilding in Devizes Museum.

The main Bath Road is rejoined at the old coaching village of Pickwick, a short mile onward. Thence in eight miles you reach Bath and the *Francis Hotel* in dignified Queen Square, the earliest of the many fine squares, crescents and parades that are so characteristic of the city.

# CHAPTER SEVEN

## *The South-Western Counties*

QUEEN SQUARE, Bath, was designed by the famous architect John Wood senior, and begun in 1728. Almost the whole of its south side, erected about a couple of years later, was occupied by the *Francis Hotel* until, in the second German War, lives were lost and half the Hotel destroyed by a high explosive bomb.

The hotel comprises six houses, all of them with early Georgian staircases, fireplaces or other decorative features. When new-built these houses were fashionable private residences; later they became lodging-houses, and eventually were united to form the hotel. Many of them were letting lodgings before the end of the eighteenth century, and to No. 6, the easternmost house of the *Francis Hotel*, Harriet Westbrook, the poet Shelley's young wife, came to stay in July 1814, after she had left her husband. In a house adjoining the *Francis* on the west side Jane Austen lodged in 1799. Indeed Queen Square like the whole of Bath is rich in literary associations.

Bath makes a good starting point from which to visit some of the old inns of Somerset and Devon, or to strike northward to see those of the western Midlands. If you go south, start with the *Royal Clarence* at Bridgwater. This is a really good example of a late Regency house, although it was not built until the Regent had become King.

It dates from the 1820's and replaced two ancient inns, the *Angel* and the *Crown*. It takes its sign from the Duke of Clarence, afterwards King William IV. When it was new it opened as the *Royal Hotel*, but a visit from the Duke shortly afterwards brought the *Clarence* into the name, and the inn still has its *Clarence Room* on the first floor which the Sailor King is said to have occupied during his visit to the house.

The *Royal Clarence* has suffered little change in the past hundred years. Its lofty, well proportioned rooms and corridors are truly elegant and valuable examples of the taste of George IV.'s days. Its spacious Assembly Room, with a Musicians' Gallery, was advertised as one of the attractions of the town in 1830, and it is interesting to note how standard is the style of decoration throughout the house, less elaborate on the top floors, but all of a type. Two "period" relics at the inn are a six-tapped, Sheffield-plated Spirit Fountain in the Bar, and the much polished brass plate in the Entrance Hall, pierced by a slot for coins and inscribed: "For the Benefit of the Bridgwater Infirmary." The arms of Bridgwater over the Ionic portico have nothing to do with the inn. They come from the town's old Iron Bridge and were placed on the portico when the bridge was pulled down in 1883. The initials are those of Robert Codrington, an eighteenth-century mayor.

Up the river Parret, which that bridge spanned, a tidal "bore" runs twice a day, and from Bridgwater's parish church tower the luckless Duke of Monmouth on a July day in 1685 watched the advance to Sedgemoor, a mile or two distant, of the Royal army that was to bring defeat to his cause and him to execution.

If you journey to Langport across the marshy moor country through Westonzoyland and Middlezoy—the "zoy" means "island" —you pass close by the battlefield of Sedgemoor, and at Langport there is an inn that hides behind an unassuming stone front some very early fine workmanship. This is the *Langport Arms*, known, until about a hundred years ago, as the *Swan*.

The house was probably once a rich merchant's dwelling and what is now the inner Lounge one of his best rooms. It has a magnificent moulded timber ceiling of the fifteenth century, and a flat-arched stone doorway of the same period. The outer Lounge, too, has moulded ceiling beams and its walls are pine-panelled in the style of the late 1700's.

Its simple mantelpiece is attractive, made of colourful stone from the neighbouring Ham quarries. The rest of the house is largely Georgian in character with old doors and deep-set window seats. The usual "Long Room" giving access to the top of the massive stone porch has been divided.

It is a charming place, full of atmosphere. In the old days it was a very busy posting inn and the house of call of the principal London to Devonshire coaches. In the early records of the town

*Gothic windows of the Abbot's Hall at the* Luttrell Arms, *Dunster.*

the *Langport Arms* as the *Swan* figures frequently. It was in business as an inn in 1650 when it belonged to the Corporation, and was the house where visiting Puritan ministers, who came to preach in Langport, were entertained. Two typical records are: "Minister's dinner and wine, to John Mitchell 17/6" and "the preacher's dinner and wine to John Mitchell 16/6"; a very lavish expenditure on the pious divines in view of the buying power of money in Commonwealth days. John Mitchell the landlord was Portreeve of the Borough in 1659.

Judge Jeffreys's grim name is closely associated with Langport. Three local men were hanged, drawn and quartered in the town as the result of his "Bloody Assize" after Sedgemoor, and a tradition grew up—not so sound as many inn traditions are—that the tragic lady whose picture hangs in the inner lounge was Judge Jeffreys's wife.

Another old posting house, but a larger one, is the *County* at Taunton, Somerset's county town, thirteen miles from Langport. The *County* again has changed its old name. It was the *London* in coaching days, one of the most important inns of the west. An old house, it was drastically reconstructed in the prosperous days of the post-chaise and coach and but little more than some Jacobean panelling, mixed with later Georgian wainscot in the office, remains of the older building. Its plain front and big porch date from 1820, so do its fine Assembly Room on the first floor, now used as the Residents' Lounge. This spacious chamber has two sets of folding doors so that it can be divided, when needed, into three rooms. A later built Assembly Room is now the Dining-room.

A modern tale of this old inn is that of its Gun Room, created recently out of the old Tap Bar. It is decorated like the Gun Room of a country house with sporting prints, cases of birds, stags' heads and old fowling-pieces, and it has become a sort of unofficial club for sportsmen and naturalists of the neighbourhood.

In striking contrast to the Georgian spirit of the *County* is the mediævalism of the *Luttrell Arms* at Dunster. You come to Dunster in twenty miles from Taunton by a lovely wooded road under the Quantock Hills and find in it one of the most delightful of little west-country towns and a superb old house. And yet once more

*The* Harcourt Arms *at Nuneham Courtenay, near Oxford, the model inn of a model village built in 1762.*
(See Chapter 8)

*The yard of the* Crown *at Amersham, an inn notable for its wall paintings.*
(See Chapter 8)

*The cobbled entrance hall of the* White Hart Royal *at Moreton-in-Marsh,*
*where the post-chaises once drove in.*
(See Chapter 8)

*An oak-panelled room at the* White Hart, *Chipping Norton, and (left) a closer view of the carved oak panelling visible to the right of the upper picture.*
(See Chapter 8)

here is an inn that has changed its original sign. This was the *Ship* when it first went into business. Incidentally it is generally a safe bet if you find an ancient inn with the name of some neighbouring family's arms that it formerly bore a simpler sign. The "So and So Arms" is a comparatively recent name, seldom earlier than the last century, although in the case of the *Ship* it had changed to the present sign in 1779. When your really old innkeeper went to the arms of the big local family for his sign, he would choose one of the charges of the shield, a lion, a star, a fox perhaps. They had to be more definite in an age when few people could read. But to the tale of the *Ship*.

The inn has grown up about a Gothic Hall erected, according to local history, by the Abbot of Cleeve, the great monastery five miles away, in the fourteen hundreds. The greater part of this hall is intact, divided by a floor into two chambers. Gothic windows light each chamber, and carved oak panels decorate the outer wall between the tiers of lights. The upper room has a hammer-beam roof, the lower one has moulded beams in the ceiling and a huge fireplace that was once an open hearth. This room was used as the inn kitchen for many years.

In the rooms of the front block facing the street is some remarkable moulded plaster decoration of the late sixteenth or early-seventeenth century. There is an overmantel in one room, extending to the ceiling, with figures in Elizabethan or early Jacobean costume, shields of the arms of France and England, and a central panel surrounded by a decorative border, depicting, apparently, the classical story of Actæon being devoured by his own dogs. In an adjoining room are the arms of George Luttrell, who died in 1629, and his wife, in the same fashion. This unusual decoration is said to be the work of Dutch craftsmen attracted to the town by the many Dutchmen engaged in its cloth weaving industry in past days.

The house came into the possession of the old Dunster family of Luttrell in 1376, whose descendant sold it with the village in 1949. In the middle of the broad street in front of the *Luttrell Arms* is the Yarm Market, a seventeenth-century relic of the cloth weaving days for which Dunster was famous. From the garden behind there are grand views of the Bristol Channel coast just beyond the foot of the hill upon which the ancient town stands.

You skirt that coast for many miles as you journey westward through Minehead and Porlock, by the edge of Exmoor, a glorious breezy road that leads into Devon. Look to your brakes if you are driving, for you have Porlock Hill to face and Countisbury Hill—1 in 4 in parts—and that fierce ascent from Lynmouth before you come to the *Crown* at Lynton, a stopping place on the way to old-fashioned Bideford.

The *Crown* is an odd inn that developed from an early, modest village ale house as the once remote Lynton grew in the last century into a tourist resort. The oldest part of the house is that of the Tap Room and the Bar at the end by the arch facing Sinai Hill. This was the *Crown* of the days when Lynton was off the map, approached only by the roughest of roads. The rest was added to it as increasing trade demanded. That began in the early years of the last century, and soon the *Crown* was one of the four chief inns of Lynton. Old guide-books tell an amusing story of those rival inns. They kept their post-boys with extra horses at the bottom of the steep hill to drag visitors' carriages up, and quarrels among the post-boys over who should claim the carriage were common. Also says one guide-book: "At Lynton, telescopes are employed at the rival houses for the prompt discovery of the approaching traveller," so keen were the innkeepers for custom.

A progressive proprietor of the *Crown*, fifty odd years ago, improved on the telescope idea. He also owned an hotel at Lynmouth at the bottom of the precipitous hill and he installed what must have been one of the earliest telephones in Devon between his two houses. In his time the *Crown's* Annexe was acquired, an old house said once to have been a farm with its yard in front of the inn.

At Lynton you leave the coast and, still skirting Exmoor for a while, come through lovely country, by Barnstaple to Bideford, that ancient Devon port of Merchant Adventurers, the town of Charles Kingsley's *Westward Ho!* At one end of Bideford's famous Long Bridge across the Torridge, in what is known locally as "East the Water," is the *Royal Hotel*, parts of which in their time have been a wealthy merchant's house, the town's workhouse and its prison.

As an hotel, the *Royal* dates only from the 1880's, but it comprises the greater part of a fine waterside mansion built in 1688 by John Davie, a merchant of the town, and the site of the *New London Inn*, which was an oldish house, despite its name, that stood at the corner. John Davie's mansion was known as "Colonial House," and most of it remains, including two very beautiful rooms. They are pine-panelled and the larger one, called the "Kingsley Room," has a magnificent plaster ceiling of festooned flowers, fruit and foliage in high relief.

Charles Kingsley's association with the room was in the early 1850's when he was writing *Westward Ho!* Colonial House then was occupied by a Bideford merchant and shipowner, a Mr. Heard, much interested in the history of his town. To his house and to this room Charles Kingsley came frequently to consult Mr. Heard's books and documents. The room was then the family drawing-room, furnished, as one of Mr. Heard's descendants remembered it a few years later, in typical Victorian fashion, its pine panels painted and grained to resemble oak.

The second of these two lovely rooms, across the landing, was the "Best Bedroom" with a Powder Closet adjoining. It too is panelled, and ceilinged in similar, though less elaborate style. These rooms are approached by a noble seventeeth-century oak staircase, and the attics above are also part of the original house. More of it still remains in the north wing and here, on the ground floor, are three of the prison cells with sliding peep holes in double-planked doors, and little grills above. The windows have been inserted subsequently and probably replaced smaller, barred ones. The workhouse preceded the prison which was in use for a short time only and was closed in 1853.

Close by Bideford are the quaint little ports of Appledore and Instow famed in Devon history, and modern Westward Ho! echoing Kingsley's fame in its name, the place where, later, Rudyard Kipling was at school and laid the scene of his *Stalky* tales. Inland a pleasant road leads by the Torridge valley towards Dartmoor by way of Okehampton to Moretonhampstead.

There is a beautifully modelled sign over the sturdy porch of the *White Hart* here, though oddly enough it is that of a hind, not a hart. The inn itself is a comfortable old place of low-ceilinged rooms and a long if uneventful history of coaching and posting times and "Farmers' Ordinaries" on Market Days. At the time of the Napoleonic Wars it was a rendezvous of French officer prisoners on parole, many of whom lived in and about Moretonhampstead. There are still many French names in the town. At the *White Hart* the old west country custom of burning the "Ashen Faggot" is kept alive. The faggot is burnt on Christmas or New Year's Eve. Made of sticks or small boughs of ash, bound tightly together, the burning was the occasion of much hospitality and merriment in past days, the snapping of each bond being the signal for replenishing with cider the mugs of the party assembled.

The last of these inns of the south-west is the *Dolphin* at Bovey Tracey a few miles beyond Moretonhampstead. Bovey Tracey is on the way to the Exeter-Plymouth main road which will take you east, west or north as your destination demands, and the *Dolphin* is worth a visit because it is an example of an old inn that deserted its original premises, took its sign to a new-built house about sixty years ago and left the old one still standing.

The house that bore the *Dolphin's* sign for centuries remains on the opposite side of the road, fifty or sixty yards nearer the town. It is an old thatched building that was in business until 1876 certainly, a commodious and busy inn, it is still remembered, with big stables and an Assembly Room, but subject to sudden floods. One old Bovey resident tells how the water came so unexpectedly into the Tap Room that he and other customers had to rush out of it. That was one of the reasons that influenced John Joll, its last landlord, to build a new house.

He built it well, in the old tradition, gave it the conventional "Long Room" on the first floor front above the porch, extensive stables about a yard, and flourished as a Jobmaster and "Proprietor of Dartmoor Coaching Trips," for many years. But its tales can but be modern: the early ones belong to the old thatched building across the way.

# CHAPTER EIGHT

## Middle England: The South

THE MIDLANDS are hard to define; the Eastern, the Western, the Northern counties impinge upon them confusingly. South only, the Thames forms a definite limit. So you may take Oxford as a starting-point for this district and see some inns on your way to it—or your ways, for these inns lie on alternative routes from London to the University city.

Begin with the *Castle* at Windsor. This is a house that displays the luxurious decorations of the latter half of the eighteenth century. It stands, possibly, on the site of an early inn the name of which is lost. But it is mentioned in 1778 when the furniture of Nell Gwynn's old house in the town was sold by her great-grandson, the third Duke of St. Albans, and "Nell's bed was bought by the landlord of the *Castle Inn*," a contemporary record tells. A few years later the *Castle* had become one of the two chief posting houses of the town, patronised by royalty and entertaining important visitors to Windsor Castle on the occasion of Courts, and similar functions.

To the *Castle*, in 1814, a cheering crowd drew the Duke of Wellington to be feasted by the Mayor and Corporation at a dinner attended by the Royal Dukes of York and Cambridge. Local newspapers tell of crowds of fashionables at the inn, come to attend George IV.'s courts, and of members of the Privy Council staying there when the Council met at Windsor.

What recent modernisation has been done at this inn is on the ground floor. On the upper floors there are some charming period panelled rooms with carved window and door frames, and in one case a really good mantelpiece. But the most finely decorated room at the *Castle* is not part of its original structure. It belongs to an adjoining private house, in recent years embodied in the inn. Used now as one of the Lounges, this room was ornately and expensively decorated in the middle 1700's. Walls and ceilings bear delicately

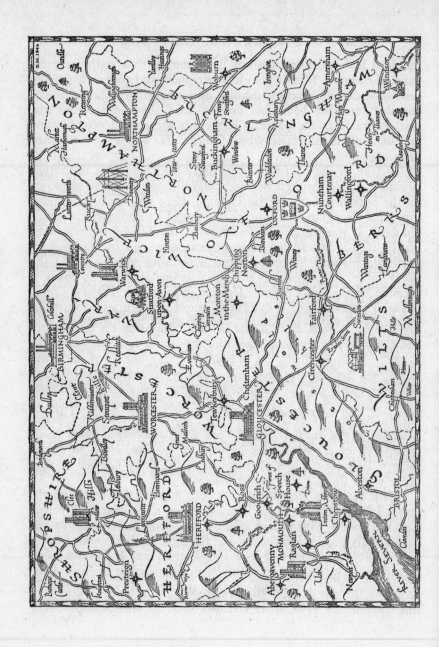

moulded leaf and floral designs in plaster, with a ceiling central panel of cherubs. It has a delightful fireplace, and door and window cases have carved wood mouldings. It is altogether a most unusual chamber, and the bedrooms on the floor above are among the best decorated in the house. Clearly this was a residence of some-one of wealth and taste when George III. was a new-crowned king.

To take in the next two inns, make for Oxford by the rather circuitous route through Reading to Wallingford, a very old town on the Berkshire bank of the Thames. Here the *Lamb* is a Tudor inn, with Georgian additions, that changed its name frequently in old days. It was the *King's Head* in 1550, the *Bell* a few years later. But by 1669 it had settled on its present name, for in that year its landlord, Silvanus Wiggins, issued a farthing token bearing the *Lamb's* sign. Wiggins was a man of importance in the town, a member of the Corporation. He was followed by Thomas Clack, father of several beautiful daughters, one of whom married Viscount Courtenay in 1762, and another, the son of Sir John Honywood, a Kentish baronet.

The oldest part of the house is the half-timber wing with overhanging upper storey bordering the Oxford road. There is woodwork there that may well have belonged to the 1550 inn. The kitchen windows have moulded mullions both on the road and the yard side, and the rooms have oak wall and ceiling beams. There is a lot of very good old furniture in the house. The Coaching Clock that hangs in the Entrance Hall is a very fine specimen indeed. It was made by John Higgs, a local craftsman, and its interest is increased by the pedigree of his family, tracing descent from Henry III.'s time, that hangs beside it.

A short eight miles farther on towards Oxford you come to Nuneham Courtenay, perhaps the oldest "model village" in England. Its story is interesting. Ancient Nuneham Courtenay was in the neighbouring Nuneham Park, but in 1765, when the first Earl Harcourt was building himself a great new mansion house there, he decided to demolish the old village and build a new one for his people by the side of the Oxford road. With it he built a brand new inn, the *Harcourt Arms*, at the Oxford end of the village, and neither inn nor cottages have changed much in appearance in the intervening century and three-quarters.

The inn, like the cottages, was originally thatched and had "a great sign hanging across the street" so a German, Pastor Moritz, recorded in a book he wrote of his travels through "Several Parts of England in 1782." Pastor Moritz came to the *Harcourt Arms* tired after a long journey on foot, in the dark of a June evening, and met with an inhospitable welcome. When he asked for a room they told him all beds were engaged and that as he had come so far he might as well walk on to Oxford. The Pastor asked for food and was told it was more proper for him to sup where he lodged. They gave him a pint of beer for ready money but refused him a piece of bread, and presently banged the door in his face. So the weary Pastor trudged on to Oxford.

Inside, the house retains many of its original features. Quite possibly it was built upon the site of a Gothic chapel, for fourteenth-century stone figures and window tracery have been dug up in the kitchen garden from time to time, some of which is preserved in the side garden. There is no record of such a place, but a man who would pull down a whole village and rebuild it a mile away would certainly not hesitate to remove some old ruins to put up his new inn.

From a student's point of view the *Harcourt Arms* is particularly interesting because it is dated to a year and still shows fairly clearly the sort of accommodation the modern, larger, village inn provided at the time.

Five miles along the road Oxford begins, but there is one more old inn of which to tell before visiting the city. It lies on the alternative route from London and involves a short detour from the direct London-Oxford road three miles beyond Uxbridge. This is the *Crown* at Amersham, a very pleasant timbered building despite its austere Georgian brick front to the High Street.

A feature of the *Crown* is its Elizabethan mural decoration. Above a fireplace in the oak-timbered Lounge the arms of Queen Elizabeth, with Lion and Dragon supporters, are painted on the wall. Traditionally they were set up to commemorate a visit of that queen to Shardeloes, a country seat on the outskirts of the

*Tudor gables of the* Fleece *at Cirencester seen from the inn yard.*
(See Chapter 8)

*An early seventeenth-century panelled mantelpiece at the* White
Swan, *Stratford-on-Avon.*
(See Chapter 8)

*The solitary* Speech House *in the middle of the Forest of Dean.*
(See Chapter 9)

*Not an early English chapel but the curious* Hostelrie *at Goodrich.*
*An example of the " Pseudo Gothic" taste of the early nineteenth century.*
*(Below) Seventeenth century plaster work of the head of King Charles I.*
*in the Bar of the* King's Head, *Monmouth.*

(See Chapter 9)

*Detail of the Elizabethan wall painting at the* Crown, Amersham.

town. An upper room has the whole of one wall painted in a design of blue, green and yellow cartouche shields divided by dark claret-coloured bands, the centre of each cartouche being veined in red to represent marble. Formerly, Mr. Francis Reader the great authority on such paintings believes, most of the walls in the principal rooms had some similar decoration. Indeed, traces were found in the Lounge but it was not possible to preserve them.

The *Crown* can claim to be one of the last coaching inns in England, for until 1890 a horsed omnibus, direct successor of the old stage-coach, plied daily from the inn to the *Old Bell* in Holborn. Then the Metropolitan Railway came to kill it.

From Amersham you regain the main coach road at High Wycombe. Oxford provides a useful centre from which to visit half a dozen other old inns all within a forty-mile radius. There is the *White Hart* at Buckingham, for instance, twenty-five miles away.

To tell a modern tale of the *White Hart* first: it has excellent asparagus beds in its big kitchen garden. Their fame is known locally. To revert to old times, Buckingham is one of the many English country towns that have been swept by fire, and the *White Hart* one of the inns that suffered. Buckingham's fire in 1725 destroyed 130 houses, left the place desolate and lost it its status as county town.

The *White Hart* is a rambling old place with changing floor levels upstairs, sure sign of many additions and alterations in the past. It was the principal posting house of the town in its day and always associated with the great house of Stowe near by, both when it was the seat of the Dukes of Buckingham and since it has become a big public school. The many-quartered arms of the Dukes of Buckingham hang in the Dining-room. Its most interesting room, as at the *Castle* at Windsor, is that of an adjacent house now embodied in the *White Hart*. This is a well proportioned front room, with deep window seats, pine-panelled from floor to ceiling. Its marble mantelpiece is of charming and delicate design. This is a room of a middle eighteenth-century house, more tastefully decorated than any of those in the inn adjoining, and unaltered, because unlike the inn it had not to modernise itself to please the changing tastes of a fickle public.

Nineteen miles north-west of Oxford is the *White Hart* at Chipping Norton; eight miles farther on the *White Hart Royal* at Moreton-in-Marsh. *White Harts* are numerous in this part of England. The sign is a very old one, taken, it is generally accepted, from a badge of Richard II., inherited from his mother, Joan of Kent, and almost as popular as the *Red Lion* sign, a badge of John of Gaunt, Duke of Lancaster (*see page 37*). Richard died in 1400 and John of Gaunt a year earlier, yet many of our oldest inns bearing these signs cannot have gone into business for fully a hundred years later.

The *White Hart* at Chipping Norton may well have put out its sign in Richard's time, for the town was a place of importance in the Middle Ages. But the oldest parts are the Tudor wings that enclose a courtyard at the back. These were galleried, and the outside stairs and stone doorway to one of those galleries may be seen in the yard and the gallery itself, long since closed, remains. There are Tudor fireplaces in the house and three of the walls of the Drawing-room are covered in Elizabethan oak panelling discovered in place behind wallpapers; the fourth has similar wainscoting brought from another part of the house.

There is an unusual and curious relic preserved in the inn, a sort of primitive automatic machine, a brass tobacco box to open which it is necessary to place a coin in a slot. It is engraved with the landlord's name on one side, "J. Goddard, White Hart, Chipping Norton," and on the other in neat eighteenth-century script:

> "A halfpenny drop into the Till,
> Press down the Spring and you may fill,
> When you have filled, without Delay
> Shut down the Lid or Sixpence Pay."

William Diston, a mid-seventeenth-century landlord, issued halfpenny and farthing tokens under the sign of his house in 1666. This William Diston a few years earlier had had to ransom his uncle, Henry Cornish, taken prisoner by the Royalists, for £6,000. His name still survives in Diston's Lane at the back of the inn.

The *White Hart Royal* at Moreton-in-Marsh has a tale of King Charles I. to tell. He slept a night there in July, 1644, when on his way to Evesham. The room which, according to tradition, he occupied is in the oldest wing of the house, bordering the Oxford road, a wing that was well over a hundred years old when the King slept there. Hanging in the room, written by some landlord of the past, are the lines:

> "When friends were few and dangers near
> King Charles found rest and safety here."

This is a fascinating old house through which to wander; it is full of odd and interesting features. Its entrance hall was once the driveway through to the courtyard. It is still cobbled and from the early moulded beams overhead one of the game hooks survives. There are unexpected little mullioned windows to be found here and there and a stretch of twisted rail balusters, and a dog gate at the foot of the main staircase. The Royal coat of arms over the front door was made for a tentmaker in the town who carried out Government contracts in the Victorian era. After his death and the closing of his business, it was bought by the then landlord of the *White Hart* as a curiosity. But the *White Hart Royal's* greatest feature is its Lounge with a huge open fireplace and moulded oak ceiling beams of the very early 1500's, all of which were hidden until revealed by restoration work.

The *Royal* of the inn's name is a comparatively modern addition; simply as the *White Hart* it was known in coaching days and for centuries before; the present building appears to contain part of a stone house of early fifteenth-century date. At one time it had a famous "gallows" sign spanning the Oxford road from a post at the inn corner to another by the Curfew Tower opposite. It portrayed a huntsman, hounds and the white hart which they pursued, strung out along the top of the cross-beam. A picture of it is remembered as hanging in the inn, but it was sold by a past landlord, and has gone—who can say where? Incidentally the "Marsh" of the town's name has nothing to do with swamps. It means "march" or boundary and probably has connection with the Fosseway, the great Roman road from Exeter to Lincoln upon which the inn fronts.

Cirencester is rather farther from Oxford, thirty-seven miles on the road to Bath. You pass Fairford on the way, where the church has one of the most complete series of old stained glass windows in the country. Or you can follow the Fosseway from Moreton-in-Marsh by Stow-in-the-Wold and reach it in twenty-three miles through the lovely Cotswold country.

In Dyer Street, Cirencester, is the *Fleece*, well named in a town made rich by the wool trade in the old days. It was a meeting-place for the flock-masters and wool staplers rather than a coaching-house. Rebuilding and alterations have made practically two houses of the old inn. The entrance to the courtyard divides them. The older, least changed part is to the left. This is full of old oak and has an interesting staircase of Elizabeth or James I.'s time. The part to the right is of later date, an early Georgian reconstruction with the Assembly Room now in use as a Lounge. The age of the house is best judged from the yard, for its front has been sadly treated in past times. There, the many gables of the older part proclaim its Tudor origin.

Paradoxically the best tale the *Fleece* has to tell is of the *Sun*, an ancient inn that once stood next door. It was a much less imposing inn than its neighbour, and to it seeking a modest inn on a September evening in 1651 came riding a party of three, a Mr. Lassels, with his kinswoman, Mrs. Jane Lane, and a roughly dressed young fellow, Will Jackson, a tenant farmer's son, travelling with them, as they explained. Will Jackson was given a truckle bed in Mr. Lassel's chamber, a contemporary writer tells. But Mr. Lassels slept in the truckle bed, for Will Jackson was Charles Stuart, already in fact Charles II., a fugitive after the battle of Worcester with a price upon his head. That tale must have been told many times, enviously, in the *Fleece*, when the king enjoyed his own again nine years later.

A short half-hour's drive through the Cotswolds from Cirencester brings you to the *Royal* at Cheltenham, the tale of which belongs to another chapter. There are tales of several other inns to be told first. Let us go farther north to Stratford-on-Avon and Warwick.

Stratford-on-Avon is, of course, dominated by Shakespeare, and the *Shakespeare Hotel*, with its nine timbered gables, is one of the world's most famous hotels. Of all the Tudor buildings in this ancient town, the *Shakespeare Hotel* is the largest and most striking. When William Shakespeare was a schoolboy, he passed this beautiful edifice daily as he went from his home in Henley Street to the little Grammar School that was held in the upper room above the Guild Hall.

It was Mr. H. E. Forrest in his book, *Old Houses at Stratford-upon-Avon* (1925), who showed the hotel to be the "Great House" built by Sir Hugh Clopton, who died in 1496. It had been generally assumed that it was erected, not as a single building, but as a row of merchants' houses. Actually, Sir Hugh Clopton died in London, but there is no sound reason for doubting that the "Great House" was his residence. Mr. Forrest, however, surmises rather curiously that this fine building, the largest in Tudor Stratford, was a great warehouse, one reason being that it has no "hall," as was usual in the mansions of that period. The "hall" of Tudor manor-houses was, however, required for the holding of manorial courts and other such purposes, when all the tenants were compelled to attend, and as the "Great House" was not a manor-house, no hall was required.

The gardens of the "Great House" were extensive, and included a burgage (or plot of land without a dwelling house) in "Chapel Street over against the Chapel on the north side." According to Mr. Forrest, the Cloptons, at some time after 1496 and before 1563, built on their land the house which was also called New Place; this was eventually sold to William Shakespeare in 1597. It has always been assumed that the "New Place" of Shakespeare was the "Great House" of Sir Hugh Clopton, but there can be no doubt that New Place, where Shakespeare lived and died, was in no sense a "great house," since it is one-half the length of the *Shakespeare Hotel*, and indeed smaller than houses in Bridge Street and High Street.

While only a small portion of the original Elizabethan structure remains at the Town Hall end, the five gables at the south end have stood through the centuries almost unaltered, except that, like other houses in Stratford, their beautiful timbers were hidden by stucco or plaster about the reign of Queen Anne, from which state they were restored in 1882. When the Town Hall end was rebuilt, the gables were constructed entirely of brick, and later alterations completely disguised their character. About 1820 a portico was erected according to the taste of that time, and this was removed in 1919, and the building restored as nearly as possible to what must have been its Elizabethan appearance. During the restoration, portions of the older gables were discovered. Though no pictures of the "Great House" as it was erected by Sir Hugh Clopton in the fifteenth century are extant, it now appears as a typical Tudor mansion.

At what precise date the "Great House" became an inn or hotel is uncertain. When the Town Hall was rebuilt in 1769, the building was "dedicated" with considerable ceremony by the great actor, David Garrick. It is supposed that he suggested the naming of rooms in the inn after the plays of Shakespeare, and opinions are divided as to whether this originated at the *Shakespeare Hotel* or at another once famous but long demolished inn, the *White Lion*. Certainly in Garrick's play, the *Stratford Jubilee* (as printed in 1774), the unnamed inn at Stratford where several scenes are set, has rooms called *Love's Labour Lost* and *The Merry Wives*. This custom has delighted visitors at the *Shakespeare Hotel* for generations, and nearly every author who has recorded his impressions of Stratford has commended its gracious pleasantry. *As You Like It* is the name of the dining-room: the little homely old-fashioned bar is called *Measure for Measure*. *A Midsummer Night's Dream* is the name of a very fine suite. Others are called *Twelfth Night,* *Julius Cæsar, Rosalind,* and *Autolycus.* And so on throughout the hotel.

In the seventeenth century the *Shakespeare Inn* as it was then called was a posting house where horses for post-chaises were privately hired; it appears never to have been a coaching house where the common or public stage-coaches called. In those days over the door in Chapel Street hung a sign bearing on both sides a portrait of Shakespeare; this relic has been removed to the head of the main oak staircase as a relic of the earlier time, and as a

*The little Gothic window in the Solar chamber at the* White Swan, *Stratford-on-Avon.*

striking specimen of the old English art of sign-painting. One side bears the inscription: "Take him for all in all. We shall not look upon his like again." With all its modern appointments it preserves its Tudor beauty, and for those who love old buildings, there is a quiet pervading beauty in the low ceilings, the white walls and the dark massive beams of oak. On these beams may still be seen the curious devices cut by the Tudor carpenters, five centuries ago, in the woods when the trees were felled—in the *Forest of Arden,* that is—to guide the builders in putting together the timber frame which they used as we use steel.

Another fine old inn at Stratford is the *White Swan.* Until the middle of the last century it had borne the sign of the *King's Head* for perhaps three hundred years, but originally the house is believed to have been that of some rich mediæval Stratford merchant. It certainly was old when Shakespeare was born and it contains an extraordinarily fine series of wall paintings illustrating the Apocry-

phal story of Tobit, with explanatory inscriptions in black letter.
The figures are shown in the costume of the mid-sixteenth century.
Experts date the paintings as between 1555 and 1565 so they must
have been familiar in the town in Shakespeare's lifetime. They are
in suprisingly fresh and good condition. They adorned the Hall or
common living-room of the ancient house and in Jacobean days
were covered with panelling, behind which they remained forgotten
until 1927. The old Hall with its rare paintings is now the principal
Lounge of the *White Swan*, although for many years it was its Bar
Parlour.

Apart from the Tobit paintings there is much of interest in this
old inn, oak beams, good panelling and fireplaces. The building
dates from about 1450, and in one of the bedrooms, which was
probably the Solar, or private parlour, of the original house, is a
curious little stone Gothic window so placed as to command a view
of the road leading into the town.

At the *King's Head*, as it was in his day, Stratford antiquaries
are satisfied that Shakespeare must have drunk, and that with little
doubt he knew the Tobit pictures well. His birthplace in Henley
Street is but a couple of minutes away and the inn was a prosperous
and popular one thoughout his lifetime.

Eight miles separate Stratford-on-Avon from Warwick. The
road is seen at its best in spring or early summer and of it an old
story is told of two experienced travellers who were asked which
they thought the most typically English road in the country. One
said that from Warwick to Stratford, the other that from Stratford to
Warwick. Warwick at the end of that road is entered through an
ancient gateway, and the *Warwick Arms* presents to the High Street
a white stone front that was described in a history of the town
published in 1815 as of " pleasing style and simple elegance."

It is a typical posting house, with two courtyards in the rear,
an eighteenth-century building in all probability successor to an
earlier inn burnt down in a fire in 1694 that destroyed most of the
High Street. The right-hand wing, from the front, is the oldest
part, a structure of about Queen Anne's time to judge from the
small-paned, thick-barred windows in some of the rooms. The rest
of the house was modernised a hundred years later. The sign of

*The* Radnorshire Arms, *Presteigne, built in 1616, and containing*
*a secret chamber over the porch.*
(See Chapter 9)

*Two views of the magnificent Assembly Room at the* Lion, Shrewsbury, *completed in* 1777, *designed by an unidentified architect in the Adam style.*
(See Chapter 10)

*The* Royal Hotel, *Llangollen, formerly the* King's Head. *The river is the Dee, and in the background can be seen the weir up which the salmon leap.*

(See Chapter 10)

*An Elizabethan staircase at the* Bull, *Denbigh, decorated with the "hand" crest of the Myddelton family.*

(See Chapter 10)

hanging grapes above the door is interesting; you see it best from the Drawing-room which is part of the "Long Room" of the inn. The best "Period" rooms are those of the Annexe, two Georgian brick houses adjoining. There are several pleasing features here, doors, chimney-pieces and grates.

In coaching times the *Warwick Arms* had a reputation for superiority. It did a very big posting trade, catering for chaises and private carriages, but the coaches stopped at other inns in the town. Reminders of those days you find in the cobbled yard where ostlers and harness-rooms yet survive, and in the farther yard the old Tap where the post-boys drank, decently distant from the superior *Warwick Arms* and its exacting customers.

One word of warning: do not be misled by the Adam decoration of the Dining-room. It is charming and well in keeping with this Georgian inn, but it is modern.

Maybe you will go north from Warwick. If so, you might take a look at the *Newdegate Arms* at Nuneaton. This inn was rebuilt in 1915 and no trace of the old structure survives. But it has interesting associations and is a house of pilgrimage for lovers of George Eliot. There the annual dinners of the George Eliot Fellowship are held. It was the *Oldinport Arms* of her books. In *Felix Holt* she makes use of an incident that took place in 1832 when, following the passing of the Reform Bill, the Riot Act was read from a window of the *Newdegate Arms* and the Scots Greys had to be called into the town to restore order.

The *Newdegate Arms* is a comparatively modern name. It was the *Black Bull* formerly and changed its sign in the early nineteenth century. Old pictures show it as a typical posting house, entered through a pillared porch and with an archway entrance to the stable-yard. Old records tell of the opening of its new Assembly Room in 1819 when, "one gent lost his hat and a second had his exchanged." The tales remain though the old inn has gone.

# CHAPTER NINE

## *Middle England: The West and Monmouth*

AT ALVESTON, the first ten-mile stage out of Bristol on the road to Birmingham and the North, is the *Ship*, a jolly little posting inn. It lies rather off our route but it can be conveniently reached either from Bath or Cirencester. It is an old timbered house of snug rooms and smuggling traditions; a busy place in coaching days. The smuggling tradition clings to a stone-flagged cellar from which a now blocked-up passage leads.

But it is an inn for all lovers of cricket to visit, for the *Ship's* cricket ground, adjoining, has been the home of the Thornbury Club for years past, and it was here that Dr. W. G. Grace learned to play the great game. The Thornbury Club still plays regularly on the ground and members of the Grace family play for it.

At Cheltenham, which makes a starting-place for this Middle England group of inns, the *Royal* is a Regency house comparable with the *Royal Clarence* at Bridgwater. It was built about 1820, perhaps a year or two earlier, and it has happily escaped serious alteration. Its period decorations are interesting. The moulded ceiling and arch of the Entrance Hall, and the slender, graceful pillars of the big bay window in a room overlooking the yard entrance, are notable examples of Regency taste. And there are others to be found about the house. Soon after the *Royal* opened, the *Cheltenham Guide* described it as a "unique establishment" that might "be ranked in point of elegance with any other Hotel in the Town," with a Coffee-room "in the London style" which was supplied daily with the more important newspapers. That "London style" Coffee-room has probably now become the *Royal's* Dining-room. The importance of the *Royal* in coaching days can be judged by the fact that it was the terminus of no less than twenty-one cross-country coach routes.

At this hotel you get a very clear idea of the sort of luxurious accommodation our forebears of the 1820's demanded, and you realise why the landlords of the older houses had so extensively to rebuild and alter their picturesque timber-framed structures. Competition compelled them to keep pace with the tastes and requirements of the travelling public.

The *Swan* at Tewkesbury, nine miles away, is an example. This ancient house was practically rebuilt in the eighteenth-century. The *Swan Hotel Inn and Tavern* it now calls itself, but it was more simply the *Swan* in 1579 when a contemporary record tells that the plague broke out in the town, "which by the good government of the bailiffs in shutting up the houses it began and ended in the *Swan Inn*." There are even earlier records, but except in the cellars and in the kitchen, where there are numerous hooks in the ceiling beams from which game and joints formerly hung, there is little to be seen of the Tudor *Swan*. It is pure Georgian and was already counted an old-fashioned house when the *Royal* at Cheltenham first opened its doors.

The *Swan's* handsome Assembly Room, now the Dining-room, has two good period mantelpieces. The central window opens on to the top of the porch in conventional fashion. Always the big coaching house of the town, the road Mails called regularly at the inn as late as 1864, and the old timbered house next door was the Coach Office.

A curious if fairly modern tale told of the inn is of one of the Corporation's Annual Dinners, held here eighty or ninety years ago, when, according to the report in the local papers, one of the dishes served was "Eland." Now eland is a South African antelope, and in the days before cold storage how eland got to Tewkesbury and why it was chosen to be a dish at this Civic Banquet is a problem that students of Tewkesbury's history are still trying to solve.

And an even more modern tale of this old inn is to be found in *Portrait of Elmbury* by John Moore. Elmbury is Tewkesbury and the *Swan* referred to in this biography of a market town is the *Swan Hotel Inn and Tavern*. Of the *Swan* Bar, John Moore writes, " Every country town has a bar like the *Swan*, but you will not find such a place in any city or suburb or village. It belongs absolutely to the small market town. It isn't a 'local,' in the sense that villages and city streets have their 'local'; it has a different atmosphere . . . You could call it a Town Club."

A very different kind of inn, the *Speech House* in the Forest of Dean, is of unusual character and history. Its situation is remarkable. It stands solitary amid the huge forest trees—mostly oaks and hollies—midway between Cinderford and Coleford. It was built in 1676 and was first known as *The King's Lodge*. It is situated as nearly as possible in the centre of the Forest on a site that had been the meeting-place from time immemorial of the Courts at which the Foresters met to settle their disputes over mining or forestry privileges and customs. Hence its name. Those customs are guarded jealously to this day and the ancient Verderer's Court met at the *Speech House* for centuries.

An even more ancient body assembles here sometimes, that of the Free Miners of the Forest of Dean. They possess certain hereditary rights of mining and quarrying which descend from free father to son, and their custom of swearing the oath holding a stick of holly in the hand is claimed by some antiquaries to be of pre-Roman origin.

The *Speech House* has been added to through the years, but most of the seventeenth-century house remains. The Court-Room where the Verderer's Court meets is used as the Dining-room. It is well proportioned, with a timbered ceiling and a raised dais where the Officers of the Court are seated. Of the many traditions that have grown up about this house is one which tells that an octagonal post in one of the rooms was used as a whipping-post for delinquent servants, another that a small chamber in the cellars was a cell in which prisoners were confined.

An unusual collection of four-poster beds has been accumulated in past times at the *Speech House*, one of them of great width. The inn keeps its dairy herd and its own poultry, so in a way is self-supporting, and both from traditions and situation is one of the most attractive inns in England.

At Monmouth, a few miles westward, are three good inns to visit. The *King's Head* in Agincourt Place has tales of King Charles the First. That he knew the house is almost certain, for he was a frequent visitor at Raglan Castle, eight miles away, the house of

his staunch supporter, the Marquis of Worcester. There is a traditional King Charles bedroom, and over the fireplace in the Bar is
a seventeenth-century, moulded, plaster panel of the head of the
King with the cypher C.R. and on either side two well-modelled
vases of flowers. This room has a ceiling of the same workmanship
and period in a design of wreaths of fruit. This plaster decoration
has been one of the sights of Monmouth since its erection, and is
referred to in old histories of the town and advertisements of the
inn, in one of which it is stated that the inn takes its name from the
head of Charles I. That is unlikely, for the house is much older than
the "Martyr King." The sign is probably that of Henry V.—Harry
of Monmouth—born in Monmouth Castle. The Charles tradition
would date from the time of Richard Ballard, a most loyal landlord
who, in 1668, issued a fine token halfpenny bearing King Charles II.'s
head with the legend "God Preserve Our Gracious King," and it
was he, with little doubt, who caused the plaster effigy of Charles I.
to be moulded.

*A trade token of the* King's Head *at Monmouth.*

The *King's Head* has a long coaching record. Heath, the local
historian, tells that an eighteenth-century landlord, William Rogers,
a "spirited character" he describes him, was the first person to set
up post-chaises in Monmouth. That was in the earliest days of
stage-coaches, and the North Mail coach was calling daily at the
*King's Head* in 1858.

Then there is the *Beaufort Arms.* This is a more recent inn than the *King's Head*. Nevertheless, it is a good example of the important coaching inn, built in the middle years of George III.'s reign as a modern luxury hostelry catering for the wealthier travellers along the great South Wales road.

It began as a humbler building, probably in the first half of the eighteenth century. "The *Beaufort Arms*," Heath wrote in 1804, "consisted of two tenements, one of which was occupied by William Green, butcher, and the other by Stevens, a dealer in corn. The inn yard was a Fives Court (the back part of the Market House serving to strike the balls against) kept by Thomas Pye. On his death, John Tibbs took the premises and converted them into an inn, adopting the Arms of the Duke of Beaufort to whom the estate belongs." Unfortunately, Heath does not say in what year this took place, but John Tibbs flourished sufficiently to retire a wealthy man, and the inn sufficiently to encourage some subsequent landlord to rebuild it in its present spacious and dignified form.

Lord Torrington gives a glimpse of the inn in 1781. He was an indefatigable traveller and in his diary on June 15th, 1781, he wrote at the *Beaufort Arms* that he was "now sitting in a mean room in this bad inn, which may be the best here." That certainly was not the present house. Lord Torrington admitted, however, that the stables were new and good and commented on the fact that there was much venison in the larders, which was said to come from local estates, but which he suspected of having been poached. He was disgruntled because there were soldiers at the inn and the officers took up too much of the time of the landlord and his staff. Lord Torrington was always a severe critic of English country inns.

A more distinguished patron of the *Beaufort Arms* in 1802, on the other hand, seems to have enjoyed himself. It was Lord Nelson, who, with a party of friends, stayed for three nights and was entertained there to a dinner by the Corporation on August 20th. This is recorded as a "sumptuous entertainment," the fare provided including a fine buck from the Duke of Beaufort's park at Badminton. Dinner was served at four o'clock. Lord Nelson made a speech of thanks to the Corporation, after which Lady Hamilton, who, with her husband, was one of the party, "favoured the Company with a

Song in appropriate words to the National Air of God Save the King, with the highest effect."

Finally, there is the *Angel* in St. Mary's Street, Monmouth. This is a smaller, more modest inn—yet possibly older than the others. And from the inn-lover's point of view it is a specimen piece, for the *Angel* has suffered very little drastic modernisation. There was a lot of reconstruction done about Queen Anne's time, and a certain amount of alteration during the hundred years that followed, but after that they have left the old house very much alone.

Its tale is of a very old inn, rather forgotten in a back street, and out-rivalled in posting days by the busier bustling *Beaufort Arms* and *King's Head*. But never quite forgotten. The commercial traveller, who knows a comfortable inn better than most of us, had made it his Monmouth home from home as long ago as 1804. Of the *Angel*, then kept by Mrs. Pugh, it was written in a *History of Monmouth* published in that year that it had "long been a house of great respectability frequented by the mercantile travellers of the Kingdom whose business connects them with the trading part of the Borough, and it is but justice to add that her kind attention to her guests has long secured her the highest praise in their good opinion."

The *Angel's* origin is uncertain. Possibly it was monastic for the inn is one of the many examples that support a general tradition that all *Angel* inns are connected with monastic institutions. This *Angel* stands across the road from the parish church, formerly that of Monmouth's Benedictine Priory. The *Angel* sign, when an old-established one, most often derived from the angel of the "Salutation"—itself an early sign discarded in Reformation days as "Popish." The present house has very old fabric left, notably in the Dining-room. But its early eighteenth-century features form its chief attraction, the rooms with deep window-seats, old cupboards and doors and the staircase. The flight to the first floor is of the middle years of George III.'s reign; from the first floor onward the heavy oak baluster rails are Queen Anne or earlier.

There is another *Angel* inn, at Abergavenny, seventeen miles along the great coach road to Milford Haven from Monmouth; that, too, stands within a few yards of the site of a monastery.

This *Angel* was one of the bigger posting houses of the road, always the "Head Inn" of the town. It was reconstructed, as such inns so often were, in the prosperous Coaching Age. The present Dining-room is a restoration of the inn's original Assembly Room, a good Regency chamber with interesting moulded fan decorations at the corners of the ceiling, and, in the Lounge, a contemporary mantelpiece. There is another nice chimney-piece in the Drawing-room, and one of the first-floor rooms has an attractive moulded ceiling. Parts of an older house survive in the cellars and about the big stableyard, where the Brew House once stood.

Another inn to see about half-way between Monmouth and Abergavenny is another *Beaufort Arms*, that at Raglan. Its original sign is unknown but it has borne the present name for a century and more, in compliment to the Dukes of Beaufort, owners of the neighbouring castle. The house is a mixture of old fabric and the "elegant" taste of the early years of the last century. The older part includes the kitchens and scullery, where there are heavy ceiling beams and rough masonry fully three hundred years old. This would probably be part of the public-house referred to in the Guide to Raglan Castle at which Cromwellian soldiers sat drinking during the siege of the castle, in 1646. A short distance from the castle, that public-house is described, and the *Beaufort Arms* is at the corner of the ancient road leading to it, and here the troopers "having alighted from their horses they sent a scout to reconnoitre who bringing them favourable news, they refreshed themselves at their ease."

In the kitchen the very large oak table still in use is known as the "monk's table," possibly because of a monkish tradition that has attached itself together with a story of underground passages leading from the cellars to the church. The origin of this tradition is not obvious, although there is evidence of blocking-up in the cellar, but inn traditions have a way of having some foundation, so here is an untold tale for some inn-lover to dig out.

Striking north from Monmouth towards Ross you follow the picturesque Wye Valley close by Symond's Yat. To the right, about half-way on the journey, is Goodrich, with one of the most

*Two old inns now united as the* Castle *at Ruthin. The house on the left was formerly the* Myddelton Arms. *The taller of the two buildings was the* White Lion, *depicted in an early nineteenth century print below.* (See Chapter 10)

WHITE LION HOTEL,
RUTHIN. NORTH WALES, M & C. JONES,
POSTING HOUSE, INLAND REVENUE OFFICE

*The remarkable beamed ceiling at the* Lion, *Buckden. The central boss of the " Agnus Dei" symbol in which its beams meet is shown below.*
(See Chapter 11)

*An example of the heraldic Inn sign. The Arms of the Duke of Bedford outside the* Bedford Arms *At Woburn.*

(See Chapter 11)

*The Open Gallery in the Courtyard of the* George *at Huntingdon.*
(See Chapter 11)

curious of inns—*Ye Hostelrie*.  At first sight it appears to be some Early-English ecclesiastical structure.  It is in fact a remarkable example of the "Pseudo-Gothic" taste of the early nineteenth century.

Local stories claim it to be an old chapel, sometimes an old chapel brought from Yorkshire and re-erected here.  Actually its Gothic appearance dates only from about 1830.  In design it resembles the neighbouring Goodrich Court rebuilt in 1823 and demolished in 1949.  The house belonged to the Goodrich Court estate and it seems certain that it was then partly rebuilt from designs by the castle's architect and altered to its present form to make a romantic-looking place in keeping with the ancient castles and monastic buildings beloved of those who took the popular "Wye Valley Tour."

Part of the house is old, of the seventeenth century probably, and this was refronted.  The other part was built at the time, and the result is striking, curious and not unpleasing.  There are records of the house as the *Hostelrie* for over eighty years past.  Probably before its reconstruction it was an inn under a less romantic sign, for its position at a junction of old roads and at the corner of a track from a very ancient ferry across the Wye is one at which an inn would have existed from the earliest times.

Four and a half miles onward you enter picturesque Ross with the *Royal Hotel* crowning the top of the hill round which your road winds.  In early days a Palace or Manor House of the Bishops of Hereford stood on the *Royal's* site.  There are traces of it still in immensely thick walls at the back of the hotel.  But the *Royal* itself was built as a luxury hotel in 1837 and remains little altered, a very delightful "period piece" of that time.

In its first years all the important coaches stopped at the house, and its huge stable-yard tells of the posting trade it carried on. The hotel gardens adjoin the famous "Prospect" laid out by John Kyrle, the "Man of Ross," in the seventeenth century, and share with it the striking view of the Horseshoe Curve of the river Wye. In the hotel's cellars, Freemasons will be interested to see a foundation stone laid by a local lodge in 1837.  Charles Dickens came to the *Royal* in 1867 to visit his friend John Forster, and it was here, after a heated argument that nearly caused a break between the two, that Dickens decided, against Forster's advice, to undertake his Lecture Tour in America. Forster foretold failure: Dickens made £19,000 out of it.

A much older Ross inn, the *King's Head* in the High Street, is a typical coaching house, always the "Head Inn" of the town, and full of old oak. Its Dining-room walls are covered by painted panelling put up in mid-Georgian days, and there are some unusual heavily moulded doors on the first floor that are a hundred years older. In August, 1822, H.R.H. the Duke of Gloucester dined and slept here while on a tour of the Wye Valley, and on leaving the inn, a newspaper of the period reports that the Duke "very condescendingly addressed to Mr. Waring (the landlord) his great satisfaction at his excellent accommodation, and politely thanked him for the marked attention which had been paid him while at the *King's Head*."

The *Swan*, yet another old Ross inn, abandoned its original premises in the middle of the last century and moved to new ones round the corner. The house which the *Swan* deserted is now occupied by a firm of wine merchants and the room bells still hang in it. It was a landlord of the *Swan*, James Barrett, who opened the *Royal Hotel* in 1837.

The *Valley*, opposite the *Swan*, is not an old inn, but a number of old houses now forming an unlicensed hotel. But its attractive garden is used by visitors to the *Swan*. The *Valley* has many Queen Anne features in its old houses, and a Gazebo, a tall octagonal garden house, giving wonderful views of the river. This is an erection of the middle 1700's and one that will please vastly all lovers of old buildings and the pleasant conceits of the Georgian age. Also there are the "Russian Doors," loot of the Crimea War, brought home to adorn one of the houses now embodied in the *Valley*. Great, heavy, handsome things with elaborate brass fittings, they had to reconstruct rooms to hang them.

The *City Arms* at Hereford, thirteen miles distant from Ross, is an eighteenth century rebuilding of an older inn on the same site. That had the sign of the *Swan and Falcon* and was pulled down about 1790 when the street was widened. The cost of the street improvement was borne in part by public subscription, but the Inn was rebuilt by the Duke of Norfolk. The house looks ill-balanced now, for in the dark days of old inns when the coaching trade died, the left-hand wing was sold and its front altered. In this wing, most of which has come back to the inn, was the "Great Room," famous in Hereford in the early-nineteenth century. Here big city functions took place, the local Philosophical Institute held its soirees, and the curiously named "Tempers Society" met. The society was so called, "from the approved temper of its members," old reference books state, somewhat cryptically. A piece of the elaborate cornice of the inn's famed "Great Room; and an early signboard are preserved in the Hereford Museum.

When the Duke of Norfolk built his new mansion he destroyed much of the original building, but preserved the fine Tudor room on the ground floor at the back, described by the Royal Commission on Historical Monuments as probably of fifteenth century date. On the upper storeys more of this ancient house survives. In the passage leading to the Bar is the gravestone of a Hereford citizen who died in Charles I.'s reign. It is one of many found beneath the house and they gave rise to a story that the *City Arms* was built on the site of a graveyard. But it wasn't. These gravestones were brought from the Cathedral Close when the house was built and used as flagstones to pave the floor—a practical if not very sensitive proceeding.

From Hereford you may easily visit the *Radnorshire Arms* at Presteigne just across the Welsh border. But only just, by a matter of a few hundred yards, though Presteigne be the county town of Radnorshire.

The inn is old, the house older, and you may be sure that the *Radnorshire Arms* is not its original name. Under the sign of the *Crown*, it was the chief inn in posting days. The date over its porch, 1616, may tell the year of its building. not as an inn but as a private dwelling for a family named Bradshaw who supported the Parliamentary cause during the Civil Wars. It is a lovely half-timbered house full of Jacobean panelling and oak beams and half-told takes of secret passages and hiding-places, and the Bradshaws.

There are some very charming rooms, some of them oak-wainscoted from floor to ceiling. The small chamber over the

porch is unusual and there are moulded beams in the ceiling of
the Bar. One of the *Radnorshire Arms* untold tales is of how a
number of mediæval armorial tiles came to the house. For many
years they formed the hearths of two of the bedrooms. Some of
them bore the name of Sir John Talbot, first Earl of Shrewsbury,
and his badge, a talbot dog. Sir John fought against Joan of Arc
and died in 1453. Others formed the "Rose-en-Soleil" badge of
Edward IV., and the arms of the Beauchamps, ancestors of Anne
Neville, who became the wife of Warwick the King Maker. What
were these doing in a Puritan's house? Undoubtedly they were
introduced later, but where they came from is unknown.

# CHAPTER TEN

## Shropshire and North Wales

THE *Lion* at Shrewsbury is a giant among old coaching inns and one that, in a way, dominated the road rather than was dominated by it. For it was due to the efforts of one of the *Lion*'s landlords, Robert Lawrence, that the great road to Holyhead was diverted from its old route by Chester and brought through the town—"the road through Wales between the United Kingdoms," as it is described on Lawrence's tombstone in St. Julian's churchyard.

The great feature of the *Lion* is its famous Assembly Room, a large room of extraordinary beauty, built about 1777 and delicately decorated in the style of the Adam brothers' work. De Quincey slept in this room once. He had come to Shrewsbury to pick up the London coach, and found the *Lion* full. But they gave him a bed in the Ballroom and he wrote a eulogistic description of it. "Of noble proportions," he described it, "lighted if I chose to issue orders, by three gorgeous chandeliers, not basely wrapped up in paper but sparkling through all their crystal branches, and flashing back the soft rays of my tall, waxen lights. . . ." He went on to comment on the unusual acoustic qualities of the room and its towering height.

Its mantelpieces, framed mirrors and its decorative scheme in which the lion, sign of the house, and symbols of music are combined, are delightful, and the room rightly has been counted one of the sights of Shrewsbury for more than a century and a half.

Another of the *Lion*'s literary associations is with Charles Dickens. He stayed there in 1838 with "Phiz"—Hablot K. Browne—his illustrator, in what was then an annexe; the little house adjoining with the balcony. Dickens wrote to his elder daughter from the *Lion*, "We have the strangest little rooms . . . The windows bulge out over the street as if they were little stern windows of a ship. And a door opens out of the sitting-room on to a little open gallery, with plants in it, where one leans over a queer old rail." That description holds good to-day.

125

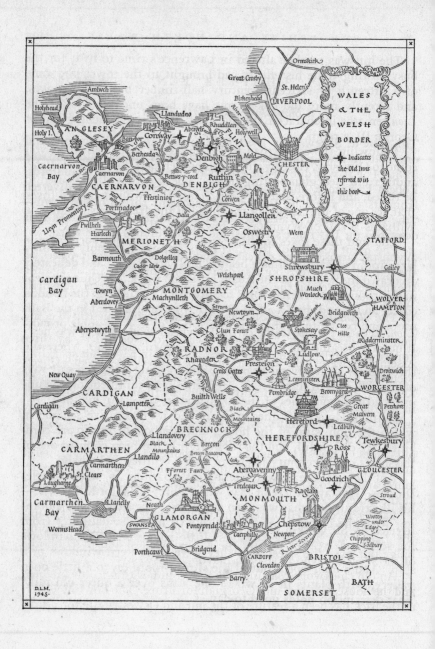

WALES
& THE
WELSH
BORDER

✶ Indicates
the Old Inns
referred to in
this book ✶

The inn was further altered in Lawrence's time to fit it for the busy posting trade his efforts had brought to the town, but some of a fifteenth or sixteenth-century half-timber building survives, and recently more old oak beams have been uncovered. But the *Lion* remains in character the big, busy, luxurious coaching inn of George III.'s reign.

Following the coach road to Holyhead for seventeen miles you come to Oswestry, close by the Welsh border, and the *Wynnstay Hotel*, another old Georgian posting house. The *Wynnstay Arms* it used to be called, and before that the *Cross Foxes*—the two red crossed foxes that are one of the charges of the shield of the great Welsh family of Williams-Wynn of Wynnstay, a few miles off.

You find these foxes together with the eagles, also borne on the Wynnstay arms, in the delicately moulded plaster centre-pieces of the ceiling of the inn's big Assembly Room, and you run up against the crossed foxes or the eagles as inn signs in all parts of North Wales.

The *Wynnstay* is a good period house, reconstructed, like the *Lion*, to cater for the traffic of the Holyhead road when it was new. It quickly became the "Head Inn" of the town, the place where the Assemblies were held and the principal travellers stayed. Queen Victoria, as Princess, was there with her mother, the Duchess of Kent, in 1832, and an amusing account of their visit is contained in an old ill-written diary. "Tom Kinaston got drunk and was turned from Mr. Knites as Post Boy," the writer tells, "Also a woman killed at Winstay there being such a crowd to see the Royal pursanges. Oswestry was the seam (same) as a wood . . . with arches across the streets and frunt of the houses all covered with laurel and ock (oak)." The "Mr. Knite" was James Knight, landlord at the time.

Earlier records tell of roasting an ox whole in front of the inn to celebrate Sir Watkin Wynn's wedding day in 1769, and of "dipping for rolls and treacle" during the annual Wakes, and of landlords of the *Wynnstay* who have been mayors of Oswestry.

An old clockwork roasting jack is still in position in the kitchen, and the house has some nice Georgian furniture. The Bowling Green at the back has been a feature of the inn and Oswestry life for nearly

200 years, and in the middle-eighteenth century the house was sometimes called the *Bowling Green*.

The Holyhead turnpike enters Wales a few miles farther on and presently descends into the Vale of Llangollen, a hilly thirteen-mile stage from Oswestry in the Posting Age. Llangollen was notorious for its bad inns in the early days of the road. There were only two of any consequence, the *Hand* and the *King's Head*, which has now become the *Royal Hotel*. The Irish patriot, Daniel O'Connell, who travelled this road frequently, had suffered both, but the *King's Head* was the first to reform itself. That was in the 1820's, and O'Connell wrote in its Visitors' Book this appreciation:

> "I remember this village with very bad cheer
> Ere the Ladies, God bless them, set this inn here
>
> But the traveller now is sure of good fare
> Let him stay at this inn or go to that 'ere
> But all who can read will sure understand
> How vastly superior's the *Head* to the *Hand*,"

The reference to the "Ladies" is to two unusual characters, Lady Eleanor Butler and her friend Miss Sarah Ponsonby who lived on the outskirts of Llangollen for years and were visited there by many of the great personages of their time. The Duke of Wellington was their close friend: Sir Walter Scott came there, and Wordsworth, who wrote a Sonnet to them. O'Connell's lines suggest that the distinguished visitors brought to the town by "The Ladies of Llangollen" caused the reformation of its inns, or of the *King's Head* at least.

After a visit from Princess Victoria and the Duchess of Kent to the *King's Head*, on the tour during which they visited the *Wynnstay* at Oswestry, the inn added "*and Royal Hotel*" to its sign, then later dropped the *King's Head*. Of the oldest inn there is little left, though of the reconstruction of the 1820's there is a good deal, and to that have been added later improvements. There are old hob grates in some of the upper rooms, and the slate tanks in the cellar where the inn cured its own bacon, within memory. But the charm

The Angel and Royal, *Grantham, one of the few remaining
medieval hostels. Here Richard III. signed the death warrant
of the Duke of Buckingham.*

(See Chapter 11)

The sign of the Golden Fleece at Thirsk. This was a famous posting house on the York to Edinburgh Road.

(See Chapter 12)

The Golden Lion, *Northallerton*. *A Yorkshire Inn.*
(See Chapter 12)

*The Black Swan at Helmsley, an ancient North Riding inn close by the
Yorkshire moors.*

(See Chapter 12)

*A painting of the kitchen of the* Beverley Arms *at Beverley, by
F. W. Elwell, R.A., in the Tate Gallery.*

(See Chapter 12)

of the place is its situation, rising straight from the river Dee close by Llangollen's ancient bridge, with good views of the mountains that enclose the Vale. Perhaps a unique attraction is the salmon ladder up the weir which the hotel's garden and many of its rooms overlook. Here in season, particularly in mid-autumn, you may see the fish leaping high into the air, three and four at a time, in their efforts to ascend the weir, fish of all sizes from twenty pounders to little fellows. It is an amazing sight, the more amazing because you may watch it as you sit in the Dining-room at your meal.

A glorious road over the Horse Shoe Pass leads from the Vale of Llangollen to the Vale of Clwyd. The road is good and the view of mountain and moorland from the summit is grand. Thence descending through a thickly wooded country you come presently to the little market town of Ruthin where two ancient inns stand side by side in St. Peter's Square. The *Myddelton Arms* and the *White Lion* were their former names, they are now united under the sign of the *Castle Hotel*.

The *Myddelton Arms* is the smaller and the older of the two. It a picturesque little house. The many gables in its steep-pitched roof gave it a Dutch appearance, and it was built deliberately in this style for Sir Richard Clough, a member of an old family in the neighbourhood, a rich London merchant and partner of the famous Elizabethan merchant, Sir Thomas Gresham, who built London's first Royal Exchange. Sir Richard Clough traded with the Low Countries and died in Antwerp in 1570. So that dates his inn to within a decade or two.

It is a snug, intimate place, rich in massive oak beams, some of which may be older than Sir Richard's house and part of an earlier building which he reconstructed, for local history claims that there was an inn here in the fourteenth century. One of its many features is a coat of arms in moulded plaster, dated 1657, on a landing wall. They are the arms of the Langford family at one time closely connected with Ruthin. Another fine piece of plaster decoration that once adorned this house is the stretch of ceiling that has been moved to the Entrance Hall of its partner, the former *White Lion* adjoining. There is a good staircase of the late seventeenth century running from top to bottom of this older inn.

The *White Lion*, which now dominates the *Myddelton Arms* and bears their joint sign of *Castle Hotel* on its front, is a couple of centuries younger. This is a house of the middle 1700's with all the characteristics of the busy coaching and posting inn of Georgian days. It has a pleasing period staircase, and the conventional "Long Room," giving on to the balconied top of the entrance porch, with painted panelled walls. But somehow, bigger and more imposing though the *White Lion* may be, the little *Myddelton Arms* will win the heart of the inn-lover.

In Ruthin, as George Borrow said, you are "treading the ground which the wild bands of Glendower had trod," for in 1400 Owen Glendower and his men raided the town and set it on fire. And you are in a town of Arthurian legend, too, for opposite the *Castle Hotel* is Maen Huail, a stone of immense age upon which, traditionally, King Arthur caused Huail, a rival in love, to be beheaded.

The road that follows the Clwyd river down its pleasant vale leads in eight miles to Denbigh and to the *Bull*, an inn with an oak staircase that is worth going a long way to see and which has a link with Sir Hugh Myddelton, who gave London its first organised water supply in the New River. Sir Hugh and his brother, Sir Thomas, some time Lord Mayor of London, were both born in Denbigh, sons of Robert Myddelton, who was governor of Denbigh Castle under Queen Elizabeth when the *Bull* was built.

The inn's really fine Elizabethan staircase has carved decoration of conventional "S.S." and hands. A "hand" was the Myddelton crest, and is a familiar inn sign in North Wales, and this decoration has reference to the family, but it provides an example of how false traditions may arise. An age that had forgotten the Myddeltons and their crest evolved a story that the hand referred to the glove trade that once flourished in Denbigh. It was an apparently obvious explanation and is still widely accepted.

Another tradition that clings to the *Bull*, which may be understood if not substantiated, is one of Doctor Johnson. A little oak chair in the house has borne the "Great Lexicographer's" name from time out of memory. It has the date 1678 carved on it, which is thirty years before he was born. But Doctor

Johnson stayed at Mrs. Thrale's house in the neighbourhood in 1774, and Doctor Johnson loved an inn. And because the little chair has had his name so long associated with it, you can but feel that there may be a connection of some kind. But what? Here is another untold tale of an old inn.

The Tudor *Bull* took in a newer house next door, probably when it began to prosper with the coming of the early coach trade. This is a house new-built about William and Mary's reign, in the late 1600's, and in it is the inn's dignified Dining-room wainscoted in the big oak panels of that time. Earlier and later work is to be found in all parts of this house; massive timbers and Georgian decoration. There is a hob-grate in a room in the Bull Lane corridor with the unusual decoration of the Prince of Wales's feathers and Masonic Square and Compasses that tells its own story. Part of the old stabling in the yard is dated 1666, and a bunch of grapes sign surmounted by three tuns, hanging over the front door, tells that the inn proclaimed itself a wine-house in other days.

The *Castle Hotel* at Conway, twenty-odd miles from Denbigh, like its namesake at Ruthin, is a combination of two old inns: the *Castle*, which doubtless had another name in its early days, and the *King's Head*. Both show a modern front to the street, a construction of 1885, but behind this there is, in the case of the humbler *King's Head*, much heavy oak timberwork of the earlier 1500's at least. The *Castle* is a coaching inn of a later period, with subsequent modernisations. But the oldest part of all is in the big stable-yard at the back where portions of the wall dividing the inn premises from the churchyard are believed to be the remains of a twelfth-century Cistercian Abbey upon part of the site of which the inn was first built.

The two inns were of very different character. The *King's Head* was a farmers' house. In its back garden was a Cock Pit which was used at times, as old inhabitants tell, by gypsies to settle their quarrels with the fists. From the little stone building at the end of the garden spectators watched both cocks and gypsies in combat. The *Castle* was the house of the "quality," the "Head Inn" of Aberconway as it used to be called. Here the Reception was held to George Stevenson to celebrate the opening of his Tubular Bridge across the Conway river in 1848, and here the coaches stopped to change horses in the stableyard.

There is a rare survival of those days to be seen in one of the existing stable buildings. It is now used as a coal store and just inside the door to the left is a small recess or cupboard. An old customer of the *King's Head* who worked in the stableyard as a boy over fifty years ago says that he was told by old men at that time that this cupboard was originally closed by an iron door, and in it Mail Coach drivers locked up their time bills, countersigned by the postmaster who supplied the change of horses, certifying the time of arrival and departure of each coach.

It is possible that more than is realised of these old stable buildings is of monastic masonry. The Abbey was removed nearly 700 years ago when Conway Castle was built and the town fortified by the walls that still surround it, for Conway is one of the few walled towns left. Later there was on its site a building known as the "Spital," probably a mediæval Guest House, and out of that the first inn may have developed. Old foundations have been found here from time to time, skeletons, a tombstone and a font to suggest tales of the *Castle's* very long ago past.

In more modern times the house has acquired a reputation for its large collection of old Welsh furniture, and for the mural paintings, mostly of Shakespearian scenes, done towards the end of the last century by two well-known artists, Dawson Watson and Bernard Ousey. A much older painting was discovered in the inn some sixty years ago. Dirty and neglected, it was eventually cleaned and proved to be a portrait inscribed "Dame Penderel 1662." Dame Penderel was the mother of the two brothers who hid the fugitive King Charles II. in the oak tree at Boscobel, and the picture, it was discovered, had been given to a former owner of the *Castle* by two old ladies, connected with the Penderel family, who lived not far from Boscobel. A photograph of the portrait hangs in the Lounge, the original is now in the town museum, close by.

# CHAPTER ELEVEN

*Middle England: East and Lincolnshire*

THE FRONT of the *Red Lion* at Luton in Bedfordshire suggests a faded Victorian gin palace or one of those dreary " Railway Taverns" run up in the middle-nineteenth century. It was actually built in 1881 by some landlord who thought he was improving an old-fashioned, out-of-date house. They had queer tastes in the 1880's.

But the *Red Lion* is a very old inn with an unimpeachable pedigree, and provides the perfect example of what should be an axiom of all amateurs of old inns: never trust to appearances. "Black and white" fronts are too often frauds; in this case a gin palace front disguises a house that was built in Edward IV.'s reign to be the Brotherhood House of the Guild of the Holy Trinity. When the monasteries were dissolved four centuries ago, it went into business as the *Lyon Inn*, and as the *Lion* or *Red Lion* it has continued ever since.

About such an old house you would expect traditions to arise, and in Luton it is said of the *Red Lion* that it was a meeting-place of the Plymouth Brethren in Henry VIII.'s reign. The story is all there, and true, if you cut out the " Plymouth," which belongs to a sect founded in 1830. So never scoff at tradition no matter how impossible it may seem to be. Dig into it: there is generally something honest behind it. But to the inn.

It has been added to through the ages but not yet restored. There are portions of an old timbered roof to be seen on the upper floor, and if the covering ceiling were removed the roof of the Brethren's Hall might be disclosed. An archway from the street leads to the inn yard. There you find survivals of the inn of Georgian posting days when the *Red Lion* had forty horses "at call" in its stables. From it you see, too, the gables of the earlier house, maybe that which the Brethren of the Holy Trinity knew.

To the *Red Lion* once belonged the house to the right of the archway, and it must have been an inn of very good standing in

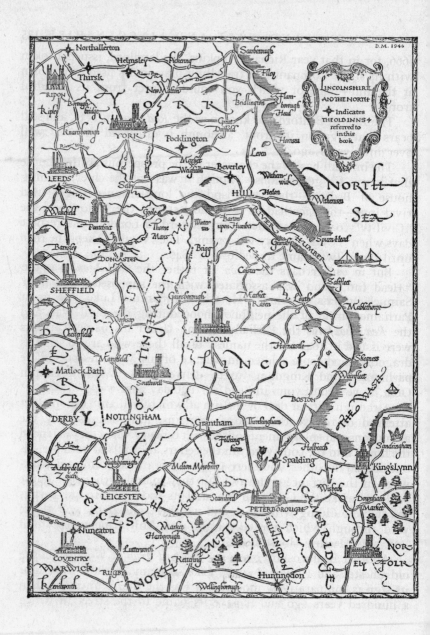

D.M. 1946

LINCOLNSHIRE
AND THE NORTH
✦ Indicates
THE OLD INNS ✦
referred to
in this
book

NORTH
SEA

Northallerton
Helmsley
Pickering
Scarborough
Thirsk
Filey
RIPON
New Malton
Bridlington
Ripley
Boroughbridge
Flamborough Head
Knaresborough
YORK
Great Driffield
Hornsea
River Wharfe
Pocklington
LEEDS
Market Weighton
Leven
Wakefield
Selby
Beverley
Withernwick
HULL
Hedon
Withernsea
Goole
Winterton
Barton upon Humber
HUMBER
Spurn Head
Thorne Mœrs
Grimsby
Barnsley
Doncaster
Brigg
Caistor
Saltfleet
SHEFFIELD
Gainsborough
Market Rasen
Louth
Mablethorpe
Worksop
NOTTINGHAM
Chesterfield
LINCOLN
Horncastle
Skegness
Mansfield
Wainfleet
DERBY
Matlock Bath
Southwell
LINCOLN
THE WASH
NOTTINGHAM
Sleaford
BOSTON
Grantham
Threckingham
Sandringham
Loughborough
Folkingham
Holbeach
King's Lynn
Ashby de la Zouch
Melton Mowbray
Spalding
Wisbech
LEICESTER
RUTLAND
Stamford
Downham Market
Watling Street
PETERBOROUGH
CAMBRIDGE
Nuneaton
Market Harborough
NORTHAMPTON
Huntingdon
NORFOLK
COVENTRY
Lutterworth
Ely
WARWICK
Rugby
Kettering
Huntingdon
Kenilworth
Wellingborough

1666, for in that year Richard Hopkins, the landlord, issued a token with its sign. Companies of travelling play-actors used to perform at the inn—none of which you could suspect from its dreadful front.

The *Lion* at Bedford was known as the *Red Lion* in 1531, and still bears that sign on its front, although it discarded the *Red* well over fifty years ago.

The inn still has all the character of the prosperous posting house that it was for generations. Though it was not the chief coaching house of Bedford—the Mails and the long-distance stages used rival inns—the *Lion* had its own short stages, the "Pilot" and the "Civility" coaches that plied from its yard to London on alternate days when the last century was young. The "Civility" kept the road until the railway came to Bedford in 1846.

But in earlier days the *Lion*, or rather the *Red Lion*, was the "Head Inn," and was associated with the supposed original of Samuel Butler's Hudibras. He was Sir Samuel Luke, the great Parliamentarian of the neighbourhood during the Civil War, and the *Red Lion* was the Parliament inn. Under his name warrants were issued in 1642 for the names "of all those who are to serve as dragoones and foote soldiers in defence of his Majesties person, ye parliament and Kingdom" to be delivered to "William Haston Gent, at ye Redd Lyonn in Bedd, on Tuesday next week."

Although a great deal of the inn at which William Haston Gent attended to receive those names remains, it is disguised by the alterations and enlargements of the next century when they extended the house into the courtyard. In the cellars are walls of both periods one behind the other, and there are an old beam and some old brickwork in the entrance archway. But they mangled the older house badly to make the Georgian inn, and its most picturesque part is the stable building with clock and weather vane at the end of the yard through which the way leads into Mill Lane where John Bunyan's Meeting House stood.

Another Bedfordshire inn is the *Bedford Arms* at Woburn on the old Chester and Holyhead road. Like so many of these *Arms* inns its sign is comparatively modern. It was the *George* until less than a hundred years ago and it gave its name to the street in which it stands. The new sign of course has reference to the Dukes of Bedford, whose vast and beautiful Park at Woburn the inn adjoins.

The familiar tale of a devastating fire is one of the many this house has to tell. The fire swept Woburn in 1724 and the original *George* with it; but when they rebuilt the inn it was on a noble scale.

The fifth Lord Torrington, who stayed there in 1789, described it in his Diary as "an Inn of Manners and Method unlike the Alehouses of Daventry or Towchester," adding, without complaint, and Lord Torrington was an outspoken critic of the inns at which he put up, "We were well treated at the *George*, but were charged as we were unaccustomed to, in the grand tavern style . . ."

The *Bedford Arms* is a splendid early Georgian inn. Its rooms are spacious and lofty, many of them panelled from floor to ceiling. In the large Assembly Room, Woburn held its regular Assemblies during the winter months, theatrical companies performed, and until not so long ago the Annual Audit dinners of the Woburn Estate were held. As an example of the best type of coaching house, it compares with the *Lansdowne Arms*, the old *Catherine Wheel* at Calne, and as a house, perhaps is a better example because it was built as an inn and not altered to please the richer, more fastidious travellers of its time. In its big stables, still remaining, a hundred horses used to stand, ready to serve the post-chaise patrons.

Little harmful change has come to the *Bedford Arms* in its two hundred years of existence, or to the graceful little red-brick Georgian town in which it stands. It is very easy to understand why Lord Torrington approved of it; such a dignified place could not be unmannerly.

In Huntingdonshire, four miles apart, are two notable inns, one on the Great, and one on the Old, North Road, close to where the two historic highways unite at Alconbury. The *Lion* at Buckden on the Great North Road is the smaller but probably an older house than the other, the *George*, at Huntingdon.

Some authorities claim that the *Lion* was originally a Guest House connected with the Palace of the Bishops of Lincoln right by the gates to which it stands. It obviously was connected with the Palace, for the great feature of the house is a remarkable timbered

*The famous kitchen at the* Beverley Arms, *Beverley, as it is to-day.*
(See Chapter 12)

*Two inns associated with the American Red Cross during the war. Above, the* White Swan *at Stratford-on-Avon, and below, the* George *at Huntingdon.*

(See Chapter 13)

*The* George, *Portsmouth, as visitors knew it before the war.* (*Right*) *The Nelson touch. All that remained of the* George *after the 1941 raid was a wall with the plaque to Nelson.*

(See Chapter 13)

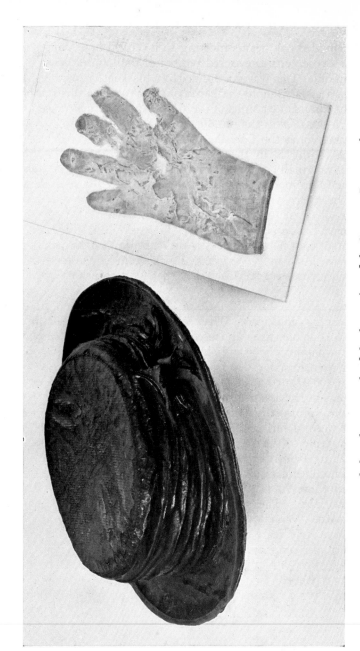

*A strange find made as a result of the destruction of the George, Portsmouth.*
*A sailor's hat and glove found in the wreckage of the roof.*

(See Chapter 13)

ceiling of moulded oak beams meeting in a central boss, carved in the shape of a rose, with the sacred symbol of the Lamb, the Agnus Dei, in the middle. This was surrounded by a black letter inscription: "Ecce Agnus Dei"—"Behold the Lamb of God." It was this symbol that gave the inn its older signs of the *Lamb*, and the *Lamb and Flag*. It changed to the *Lion* in the middle years of the last century and is still locally known as the *Lion and the Lamb*.

This fine ceiling is in the oldest part of the house, now the Lounge, but originally the Hall of a building erected about 1490. The Historic Monuments Commission described the house in detail and stated that there were two wings running back from this main block. One of these wings has been rebuilt, the other, facing Church Street, contains much of the old work. But the Hall is the most interesting portion, apart from its ceiling. It has an open hearth, partly closed now, with a chimney beam of ten-feet span, moulded and chamfered and carved with rose decorations at each end.

The house tells the familiar tale of later alteration in its many eighteenth-centry additions. They even divided the Hall into separate rooms at one time and used the open hearth as a kitchen fireplace. But happily the grand old chamber has now been restored to much of its original appearance.

The *George* at Huntingdon is a curious mixture of old and new. Most of it was burnt down some seventy years ago and was rebuilt in the gaunt, uninspiring style of the hotel of that time. But fortunately the inn-yard escaped the flames and there you see the very rare example of the open gallery running along one side, with staircase leading from the yard itself. The gallery is supported by posts with moulded capitals and bases, and the bedrooms that lead from it and those in the other old wing facing the yard have timbered ceilings. These wings date from the seventeenth century, but the *George* was in business in Henry VIII.'s time. It was sold in the early years of Elizabeth's reign to Henry Cromwell, a member of an old family of Huntingdon brewers, probably the grandfather of Oliver Cromwell, who was born close by the *George*.

The *George* was a famous posting and coaching house until the railways came to bring disaster to the old inns, and one of the many tragedies of that time was played here. Tom Hennesy, perhaps the finest whip in England, for years driver of the Stamford "Regent," known and idolised along every mile of the road between London and Stamford, had to come down to driving a two-horse omnibus between the *George* and Cambridge when coaching died. A relative, William Hennesy, was landlord of the inn then, and it must have been a sad fall for a man of whose skill and debonair ways a hundred anecdotes were told, and one who had driven the famous "Regent" from the *George* and *Blue Boar* in Holborn eighty-nine miles down the North Road one day and eighty-nine miles back the next, for years. But the 1840's are full of such stories of disaster to man and inn.

You come upon the tale of fire again at the *White Hart* at Spalding on the old Boston and Grimsby turnpike that leaves the Great North Road at Norman Cross thirteen miles beyond Huntingdon. The *White Hart* was badly damaged by fire and reconstructed in 1714.

Spalding is in the bulb-growing country, a pleasant "Dutch-like, canal town," as Lord Torrington described it when he stayed at its "good inn," the *White Hart*, in 1790. In early spring the surrounding country presents an extraordinary sight. Great wide streaks of brilliant colour from tulip and hyacinth blooms score the fields as though painted by some titanic brush. The journey to Spalding is worth the making just to see those colour-splashed fields.

The *White Hart* is one of the inns that probably took its sign from the badge of Richard II., for the first record of it is in 1377, the year in which the king was crowned. They must have rebuilt the old place within the following hundred or so years, for much good early Tudor carved and moulded timberwork escaped the 1714 fire and is exposed in many of the rooms. Then came the reconstruction that gave the house the Georgian character it has to-day.

Old tradition says that Mary Queen of Scots lodged for a night here on her sad journey to Fotheringhay in 1586, and that the "Crown Room" was that which she occupied. The "Crown Room" is part of the later "Long Room" of the inn, facing the front. But an ancient carved beam remains there that would have decorated an important chamber at the time when the unhappy queen came to Spalding, and the tradition need not be discarded.

Robert Rishton, one of Cromwell's Ironsides, was landlord of the *White Hart* in the middle 1600's. He issued a trade token with the *White Hart's* sign in 1666. Fifty-odd years later there was a duel fought in the inn; a man was killed, and what his fellows thought of him may be judged from the epitaph on his tombstone in Spalding churchyard. It reads:

> "Here lies a man of mickle fame
> Who lived by sword and prize
> And died by the same."

The upper part of an eighteenth-century staircase remains, and there are many fragments of old panelling in various parts of this very pleasing Fenland inn that has been offering hospitality to travellers for nearly six hundred years.

But even the *White Hart's* pedigree is overshadowed by that of the *Angel and Royal* at Grantham on the Great North Road. Its story goes back for over seven centuries, and it is one of the few remaining mediæval hostels in England. There is record of it in 1213. It belonged to the Knights Templars then and it entertained King John in February of that year. That was two years before Magna Charta was signed. In the following century the house was rebuilt, and the entrance archway leading to the yard dates from that time. Upon its hood moulding are carved the heads of King Edward III. and his Queen Philippa. Above it, of rather later date, is a lovely oriel window supported by a bracket of the inn's sign, a gilded Angel holding a crown. The rest of the front of the house is of middle fifteenth-century craftsmanship.

This front block is all that is left of the very old house. The wings at the back were rebuilt in the Coaching Age, when the *Angel* was among the busiest and most important inns of the North Road. The great room that runs the length of the old part is a historic one. It was known as the State Room, the King's Room or the Chambre du Roi, and in it on October 19th, 1483, having sent to London for

*The gilded sign of the* Angel and Royal *at Grantham.*

the Great Seal, Richard III. signed the death warrant of his kinsman, Henry Stafford, second Duke of Buckingham.

The *Angel's* charming fifteenth-century oriel windows have carved stone ceilings, one on the ground floor displaying "a pelican in her piety" that is feeding her young with her own blood. The *Royal* was added to the inn's sign comparatively recently. It was simply the *Angel* until the nineteenth century. One of its landlords who died in Queen Anne's reign charged the inn with the annual payment of forty shillings for the preaching of a yearly sermon against drunkenness. The sermon is still preached each Michaelmas Day and the owners of the *Angel* pay for it.

Nottingham, twenty-three miles from Grantham, has a queerly-named inn, the *Flying Horse*. Whether this sign derives from mythological Pegasus, or from the more homely flying horse, which was a primitive form of roundabout that provided much of the fun of a mediæval fair, is a matter of debate. But Nottingham's *Flying Horse* stands close by the wide Market Place, famous for centuries for its annual fair, and that may provide the answer.

It is a Tudor house, erected on the site of a mediæval one, and it has been an inn for about four hundred years and probably longer. A few years ago it was threatened with demolition by the local authorities on the plea of "improvements." But the old inn was saved at the expense of much reconstruction. The front was rebuilt most happily. It follows closely the design of an early front of the house as shown in old pictures. In the course of that reconstruction much hidden Tudor work was exposed, so that on the whole, though some old parts had to go, the *Flying Horse* has not suffered by the alterations.

Like many of Nottingham's ancient houses, the *Flying Horse* has most capacious cellars, two tiers of them, cut in the native sandstone. There is more subterranean accommodation here than can ever have been needed by an inn. Possibly it was part of the mediæval building that the first inn replaced. The cellars have never been thoroughly investigated and they are undoubtedly of great age. A relic of that former house came to light during the recent construction of a garage at the back. Some seven feet below street level a domestic mortar of the fourteenth or fifteenth century was found in a layer of sand. It is now displayed in the house.

The *Flying Horse* in Georgian days was the townsman's inn, much used by the actors of the time, and the Tory house of Nottingham, with many tales to tell of hard and bitterly fought elections. That fine old sportsman, Thomas Assheton Smith, made it his political headquarters in 1818 when he stood for Nottingham and was defeated by only twelve votes after an eleven-days' fight.

Paul Bedford, the great comedian, was a frequenter of the inn, and his signed portrait inscribed in 1849 " To the Flying Horse Malpas," hangs in the Hotel Bar and preserves the name by which a famous landlord, William Malpas, was known locally. As well as running the *Flying Horse*, he was a prosperous iron and steel merchant.

These simple tales seem trivial compared with that grim historic one the *Angel* at Grantham had to tell. Yet contrast is so essentially a part of the story of the English inn. To it through the centuries, rich and poor, king and tinker came, as they still come, under the same roof to satisfy the common human need of rest and refreshment.

There is one more inn of Middle England of which to tell, the *New Bath Hotel* at Matlock Bath. The *New* refers to the bath, not to the hotel, and the "new bath" is a medicinal spring discovered in the middle 1700's a short distance from the original spring, found and exploited some years before. That became the "old bath" then. It too had a hotel, but that has ceased to exist.

The *New Bath* developed from a number of lodging-houses that were quickly run up about the new-found spring. When they built the present hotel in the latter part of the eighteenth century they enclosed this new bath in the house. It is a biggish thing, into which you may dive and swim. From its surface a thin steam rises, for the water's temperature is sixty-eight degrees. This water is always running, in at one end and out through a long tunnel at the other to empty itself into the river Derwent. Its curative virtue is in the treatment of rheumatism, but it possesses the curious quality of petrification. When sprayed for a period on any object it deposits on it a covering of lime.

The *New Bath's* tale is largely that of the idle life of a popular Spa. It was a gay place in late Georgian and Victorian times, and a luxury hotel well built and decorated in the taste of the period. It has been enlarged, but in the older part are many examples of that taste: old doors and grates and mantelpieces. One of its attractions in the old days was an enormous lime-tree that grew in the garden. Its branches covered an area of 330 feet in circumference, and towards the end of its life were supported by numerous stakes. Romantic visitors wrote poems about it.

Indeed versifying seems to have been a popular pastime at Matlock Spa. A guide-book of 1835 quotes some lines that were scratched on a window by a diamond at the *New Bath Hotel*. They tell of a romance, the end of which we can never know. But their writer possessed a sense of humour. He wrote:

> "The bright betwitching Fanny's eyes
>   A thousand hearts have won
> Whilst she, regardless of the prize,
>   Securely keeps her own.

> Ah! what a dreadful girl are you
> Who, if you ere design
> To make me happy, must undo
> 9 9 9."

The *New Bath* has two baths now. There is an open-air swimming pool in the grounds, of the same thermal water, gently steaming. It has water-chutes and diving-boards. Fanny and her nine hundred and ninety-nine suitors would have loved it.

# CHAPTER TWELVE

## *Some Yorkshire Inns*

YOU EXPECT to find great posting inns on the old coach roads to the North. There are two typical ones on the turnpike from London to Edinburgh by way of York—the *Golden Fleece* at Thirsk and the *Golden Lion* at Northallerton.

The Thirsk inn, though an old one, came to its greatest prosperity about 1815, and portraits of the father and son who helped to make it famous still hang on the staircase of the house. In that year the landlady of the *Three Tuns*, then the big posting house of the town, retired, handed over her business to a relative, George Blythe, and set him up at the *Fleece*. Blythe bought adjoining property and enlarged the inn. In 1828 he died. The *Fleece* passed to his nephew, John Hall, and to quote Edmund Bogg, a local historian of the last century, "George Blythe and John and William Hall, the latter two father and son, built up the reputation of the *Fleece* until it became the most notable coaching house between York and Darlington."

Blythe's addition to the house is obvious in the taller building by the yard entrance. The original house, with its noble Golden Fleece sign hanging above the entrance, is older. This was the inn which the Newcastle Courant in 1726 advertised as the office for registering deeds of conveyance for the North Riding; "Mrs. Lowery's *Fleece Inn* at Thirsk," it described it. And it was an old house then.

There is a good deal of oak about the place that was put up a hundred years and more before Mrs. Lowery's time, but its early Georgian details are of greater interest. Set in a once wide open hearth, spanned by a twelve-foot chimney beam, is a charming mantelpiece of the Adam period, and the Writing-room ceiling is of not later date than Queen Anne's reign.

In the heyday of the road the *Golden Fleece* kept fifty or sixty horses in its stables to work the coaches alone. Reminders of those spacious days are the great inn-yard and its now deserted stables, the Coaching Clock by a local maker, and the amount of good old furniture the inn has kept. There are many paintings of horses in the inn, one of which is attributed to J. F. Herring, the famous animal painter who was once a Yorkshire stage-coach driver. The inn has still a weekly Market Dinner, and Yorkshire pudding is always part of its bill of fare, as it has been for generations past. But strangers are not admitted; only the local farmers may sit down to that hearty meal.

Northward from Thirsk the next change of horses the coaches made was at the *Golden Lion*, Northallerton. This is another grand Georgian inn with vast stables bordering a yard that runs a hundred yards and more back from the house. In the days of Northallerton's Horse Fair, horses were run up and down this long yard to show off their paces to prospective buyers.

Francis Hirst, who was landlord of the *Golden Lion* in the early 1800's, had the contract for supplying teams for the great coaches along the stretch of road from Thormanby, fifteen miles south, to Enter Common, eight miles north of his inn, and to have had a practical monopoly of post-horses in the district for many years.

The *Golden Lion* had a reputation for high charges in those days. It was referred to under the fictitious name of *Black Swan* by the Rev. Sydney Smith, wit and man of letters of the early nineteenth century. Writing to Lady Grey he warns her "not to set off too soon (from London) or you will be laid up at the *Black Swan*, Northallerton . . . and your bill will come to a thousand pounds, beside the waiter, who will most probably apply for a place under Government."

John Wesley may have been here. A local history records that he preached at the *Golden Lion* on Easter Sunday, 1745. In his Journal he says only "In the evening I preached at the inn at Northallerton." But possibly it was to a smaller inn calling itself the *Old Golden Lion* that he went. The point is uncertain.

The inn's sign above its wide fluted pillared porch is a notable one. It is the most benevolent of lions this, that has regarded so many generations of travellers coming and going to and from the old inn. He almost smiles a welcome. Inside, the house is good earlyish eighteenth century, its front rooms with deep window-seats and small-paned windows. You find old grates and old doors in many of the rooms, and a locally-made Coaching Clock, as it should be, in the Hall. There is ancient masonry and Tudor brickwork in the cellars to tell of an older house demolished when they built the present one close on two hundred years ago, and, bar essential improvements, nothing much later than 1850 in its fabric.

The old Assembly Room just inside the archway is still used for dances and dinners. The post-boys' quarters above the stables remain, though they have been restored and turned into staff rooms. Formerly there were horse-shoes nailed to some of the loose-boxes as relics of Northallerton's Race Meeting, founded in 1765. They were the "plates" of race-horses stabled here. The old pump and stone water-trough hark back to posting days when every one of those many stables in that long yard was full, and despite the garages you find there now, the motor car seems an intruder in this yard where the post-horse reigned supreme for so long.

At Helmsley is another old North Riding inn, the *Black Swan*.

You reach Helmsley from Thirsk, climbing a long steep hill, Sutton Bank, to the breezy moors of the Hambledon Hills half-way on the thirteen-mile journey. Or you may go round by Coxwold and see Shandy Hall, where Laurence Sterne wrote *The Sentimental Journey* when he was Coxwold's vicar, and visit Byland Abbey before you come to Helmsley Market Square and the *Black Swan*, an inn that has grown up in a haphazard sort of way.

It looks younger than it is. It needs its original roof of heavy stone slabs, such as you see from the inn-yard on an ancient house adjoining, to give it its true dignity. For there is some very early work in the place; rough stone walls almost a yard thick, and sturdy oak ceiling timbers dressed by the adze that must be four hundred years old. These remain of a house that was standing when the pack-horses laden with wool came down from the neighbouring moors and roads were rare round Helmsley.

It was modernised, of course, in coaching days, and has all the characteristics of that age, together with some earlier ones that do not belong to it. The Jacobean panelling in the hall, for instance; that came from the Parish Church when it was rebuilt about 1860. And the stone Tudor doorway of the cellar entrance. That must have been imported from the sixteenth-century wing of Helmsley Castle. The big open hearth of the Lounge belongs to the original house and it has only recently been uncovered. This room was a stone-flagged Tap Room within the memory of old customers.

The *Black Swan* was always the " Head Inn " of the little town and the only one noted as a posting inn in the old Road Books. Jury Dinners were held there, and the Annual Rent Dinner of the Duncombe Estate tenants. Some of the pewter plates and dishes in the Lounge were used at this function.

At the back, approached from Swan Lane, is a large yard, surrounded by old stone-built stables, and a big peaceful walled garden, with a rockery partly composed of carved stone that has been taken in the past from the castle. The inn is fortunate in its situation, for the moors lie close behind it, and in a few minutes by car you may be on a rough track through the heather, clean away from the world.

About the *Feathers* at Pocklington, thirteen miles from York in the East Riding, a first-class political squabble arose in 1834. The *Feathers* was the Tory inn, and to it came Lord Brougham, Lord Chancellor of England, his daughter and his private secretary early one morning. They were travelling by chaise to Hull. Lord Brougham complained that he was improperly received and the local press waged war.

The Whig papers, supporting the Lord Chancellor, claimed that he had been insulted, shown into a public room, unswept, undusted and without a fire, and that no breakfast awaited him although he had notified the landlord of his coming. One journal stated, rashly, that there were no post-horses at the *Feathers* or any other Pocklington inn.

The Tory press, in arms for the landlord, claimed that he had received no intimation that Lord Brougham desired breakfast, he had only been notified that he would change horses at the inn at a certain hour. Although the Lord Chancellor arrived two hours before his time, the horses were ready, and the party shown into the best room.

The battle raged hotly for a while, but the *Feathers* won. The rash journal that complained of the lack of post-horses had to withdraw. It published this recantation, "It is well known to all travellers through Pocklington that at the *Feathers Inn*, post-horses have been kept for the last half-century and we understand that there is no more accommodating establishment in the East Riding."

And there the matter ended, though it is said that Lord Brougham never entered the town again.

Lord Brougham would have found the *Feathers* a modern house reconstructed within the past ten years or so. To-day, a hundred-odd years later, it has the same character, although there are parts of a much older building left. Oak rafters and moulded beams in the office belong to the sixteenth century; the passage leading to the kitchen, with meat and game hooks still in the ceiling, is of the 1700's. So is the window of the still-room that probably once lighted a Georgian Coffee-room.

The *Feathers* was a great market house in its time, and a hunting inn, which accounts for its very extensive stables. One of its former landlords used to farm, and the top yard of the inn was his stockyard. The Feathers Field behind the house was a busy place during Pocklington's old May and Martinmas horse and cattle fairs.

But all that is past. Pocklington is just a quiet little country town, with only dreams of the busy times that used to be when the *Feathers* was a century younger.

Fifteen miles on towards Hull the main road passes through a fifteenth-century gateway, the ancient North Bar of Beverley, and leads in a hundred yards or so to the last of these inns, the *Beverley Arms*, opposite the great town church of St. Mary.

The *Beverley Arms* is a good place to come to at the end of a journey, a comfortable red-brick Georgian house with the usual tales to tell of earlier buildings that it has replaced. Until about 150 years ago, it was the sign of the "Blue Bell" that hung before this old inn. The *Blew Bell*, old deeds call it, and late eighteenth century prints show a painted Blue Bell suspended from a gallows sign extending in front of a tile-roofed house. This house looks as though it had been built somewhere about the very end of the sixteen hundreds or in the earliest years of the next century.

But before the end of the seventeenth century there were big alterations at the *Blue Bell*. Its main block, facing the street, was reconstructed and modernised in the early 1790's and the old sign was abandoned in favour of the new genteel one of *Beverley Arms*.

Record implies that the *Blue Bell* was Beverley's most important inn in 1666. In that year, Sir William Dugdale, who became Garter King at Arms, held his Herald's Visitation at the *Blue Bell*, and there came to him from miles around all those titled folk and gentlefolk who wished correctly to register their coats of arms and their pedigrees with the Herald's College. Only Beverley's best inn would have been chosen for such a purpose.

Twenty-three years later, a lease of the "Blew Bell" describes it as formerly of two tenements, which suggests that the inn had formerly been enlarged. And it was apparently then that the inn's noble kitchen was built.

This is a big and most attractive room, stone flagged, with a great window giving on to the inner yard—the *Beverley Arms* has two yards—and one side entirely occupied by a range of arched fireplaces, surmounted by a crenellated cornice. There are five of these fireplaces. The two larger were originally used for cooking, the three smaller ones for coppers and other culinary or household purposes. This elaborate kitchen equipment is most rare, and if it were usual in the great inns of the period, very few, if any, other examples of it survive.

To-day only two of the five fireplaces are in use, and above each of these large hearths parts of the fittings of the old roasting-jacks remain. The *Beverley Arms* kitchen has been painted more than once by Mr. F. W. Elwell, R.A. One of these pictures hangs in the Tate Gallery, London, and another in the Walker Art Gallery, Liverpool.

To the street, the *Beverley Arms* presents a plain front of mellow, dark brick, entered through a sturdy porch supported by stone pillars with fluted capitals. There is a gracefully designed fanlight over the door which is the work of the 1790's. Above the porch is a railed balcony, reached, as is customary, from one of the windows of the Long Room on the first floor. This is the room in which big functions were held in past times and, from the balcony, as long as

Beverley can remember, the Tory candidate has addressed meetings
and appeared to speak to the crowd below when he was elected. The
old custom was carried on until the boundaries of the Beverley
division were altered in 1948.

# CHAPTER THIRTEEN

## *The Inns in Wartime*

THESE TALES of old inns would not be complete without some reference to the part they have played in war. The inns have survived because of their ability to adapt themselves to the ever-changing pattern of the country's life, and it is natural, therefore, that they should have been as much a focal point of community life in war as they are in peace. The inn, as a lodging house for travellers, houses any one whose business takes him along the high roads of the country, and in war many of their guests will have been soldiers or sailors, from the rank and file to the very great whose names live still in our history books. The old *George* at Portsmouth saw Lord Nelson during his last few hours in England. From the side door of this now vanished inn the greatest admiral of our naval history was smuggled out to embark at Southsea for his flagship, *Victory*; he was bound for Trafalgar and death. The *Dolphin* at Southampton knew the great Wellington, and in the First World War, Earl Haig, then a general, used this same inn as his headquarters before embarking for France with the Expeditionary Force.

But it is not only of the great that we should think when we consider the part played by our inns in war. Think of the men who have dropped into these inns casually for a mug of home-brewed ale or a night's lodging, nameless men whom history only remembers as so many thousand who fought on such and such a field. Pistol, Nym and Bardolph, those representatives of the great mass of armed men that do the fighting—where did Shakespeare have them assemble? In a tavern in Eastcheap. Tavern, alehouse, inn—they have always been the rallying points when our island has been threatened. What tales some of these old inns could tell of the more violent chapters of our history! Some of the inns I have written of were standing in the days of King Hal, and walls that you can still see may have heard tall tales told by the veterans of

Agincourt. If only those old walls could talk! In the bars and courtyards of those half-timbered Tudor inns will have gathered the militia when they rallied to Queen Bess as the Armada sailed up the Channel. Other old inns will have seen history in the making during two civil wars—the wars of the Roses and the bitter struggle between the Royalists of the King and Cromwell's Parliamentarians. The building that was once the *Star* at Oxford, for instance, was the headquarters of Fairfax when Cromwell's forces occupied the city. Cromwell's soldiers often repaired to the *King's Head* in Monmouth for ale during the siege of the neighbouring Raglan Castle, and the great Protector himself would stay at the *Saracen's Head*, Great Dunmow, where the landlord of the time was an ardent Parliamentarian. And later, in Anne's reign, men came back to their favourite bars or stopped at inns along the road on their way home and talked familiarly of the names of foreign places that had become household words—Blenheim, Oudenarde, Malplaquet, and of the great general who had led them, ancestor of our own Churchill, the Duke of Marlborough.

But it is not only our soldiers who have made the walls of our ancient inns ring with strange oaths and stranger stories. As the inn was often the recruiting centre for the local militia, so it was often the place from which the Navy drew its seamen. The infamous Press Gangs reaped their best harvests from the inns along our coasts, and many a man was press-ganged from his favourite inn to return after several years afloat with tales of strange seas, strange peoples and storms and famous battles. If only those walls could speak of what they have heard! But often some historical association will set one's imagination wandering down time and a picture will, form in the mind of the inn as it used to be and the people who were there and the battles they talked of.

But it is not always necessary to *imagine* how the talk has run in these inns during war, for at no time in our history have the inns of Britain played such a full and useful part in war as they did in the last war. In their bars gathered pilots taking a night off to rest their nerves during the Battle of Britain, soldiers, bitter and weary, back from Dunkirk and Dieppe, men in uniform who had ranged the Seven Seas, who had been marooned for days in open boats, who had seen the inside of prison camps in half the countries in Europe, and in the Far East, men who talked of disasters and yet still had the courage and the strength to go on fighting and men who talked of victories and told of great chapters in the long story of our greatness. These stories are still fresh, still there to be retold by people who heard them with their own ears to those who are interested.

And never at any time, since the inn became a part of the life of the country, did it play such an active part in war. The Local Defence Volunteers, later named the Home Guard, and the other civil defence organisations watched and waited in the taprooms and bars of our inns, year after weary year. And the inn itself came into the front line for the first time in its life. In the days of the London blitz, I remember everybody commenting on the tendency for the bombs to single out churches and inns. The bombs were, in fact, quite indiscriminate. But because the church and the inn were symbols of community life, their destruction was more noticeable.

It was not only in London and the big cities that the inns were damaged nor did the bombs respect the antiquity of buildings. Of the hundred odd inns mentioned in this book, thirty were damaged during the war, some on more than one occasion. And though the inns that were destroyed, like the *George* at Portsmouth, were mainly in the larger towns, the tale of damaged inns spreads far and wide across the country—the *Francis*, Bath; the *White Hart*, Braintree; the *King's Head*, Rochester; the *White Hart*, Spalding; the *Dolphin and Anchor*, Chichester; and the *Beaufort Arms*, Monmouth, to mention but a few. Fortunately, in most cases, the damage was not great. Up and down the country, the inns licked their wounds and kept open house. But there are some sorry gaps. Apart from the *George*, Portsmouth, two inns I was sorry to see go were the old *King's Head*, Coventry—though I was glad to hear that the fine effigy of Peeping Tom had been preserved in safety, the night porter going back into the damaged building to rescue it— and the *White Hart* at Newmarket, which had some fine tales to tell of the racing world.

The destruction of the *George* produced an interesting relic—

an old-type sailor's hat and tattered white glove.  Presumably they
were lodged in the rafters during some pre-embarkation party, for
they were found in the debris of the roof and prior to the bombing
no one had known of their existence.  They date from about 1875.
Rather strangely—and fittingly—the wall by the archway through
which Nelson passed for the last time in 1805 remained standing
after the explosion and, with it, the plaque recording the event.

Some of these old inns found strange guests thrust upon them
during the war.  Not long ago, everyone would have laughed if
you had suggested that an American doughnut-making bakery
would establish itself in the courtyard of the *George* in Huntingdon
where the stage and post horses used to stamp and whinny.  But in
war many strange things happen.  The *Bell* at Sandwich, for instance,
had an even stranger guest—an anti-tank gun established itself
in one of the bathrooms.  The *Royal Hotel* at Bideford held many of the
secrets of the Normandy landings.  Throughout the war high-ranking
and specialised officers of both services and ministries were quartered
here for discussions in connection with Combined Operations
Experimental Work.  An official plaque, commemorating this, will
be found on the wall of one of the rooms.  Radar experts were to
be found at the *Crown and Castle*, Orford.  The American Red Cross
took up their quarters at the *White Swan*, Stratford-on-Avon, and
A.T.S. drivers took over the Adam Ballroom of the *Lion* at Shrewsbury as a dormitory.  The *White Hart* at Salisbury was for a time the
headquarters of Southern Command; the *Pembroke Arms*, Wilton,
was an officers' mess; and the *Methuen Arms* at Corsham saw a good
deal of activity when that great underground aircraft factory was
being constructed.

And so the tales go on.  There can hardly be an inn in the whole
country that has not some tale of the last and biggest of our wars
to tell, some scar to point to, some face remembered that will never
again order a pint across the bar.  The *Castle and Ball* at Marlborough
will remember the American Airborne troops and the *Star* at Alfriston
the tank crews and artillerymen who practised on the Downs above
the village.  The *Dolphin and Anchor* at Chichester will remember
some of the Canadians who went on the Dieppe raid, the *Swan* at
Lavenham those gay and gallant pilots who wrote their names on

the walls of its bar. The old inns of the south and east of England will have many tales to tell of blitzes, flying bombs, and famous fighter pilots of the R.A.F. And in any of the inns around the coast, like the *Royal Fountain* at Sheerness, you will find tales of the Navy, and people talking of their sons and husbands somewhere out across the seas.

An inn is an exciting place—its atmosphere is compounded of so much that is personal to each age through which it has lived. In these old inns, when you reach your bedroom at the end of a long journey, think for a moment of the thousands of travellers who came to it before you, from horseback or chaise, or coach or station cab, into the same room, with different wallpaper, or paint on the panels maybe, shutting the same door, looking from the same window, feeling just as peevish and just as wishful for a drink perhaps as you do. Men and women of divers classes of life; some who called a James or a Charles their King, more, who, as you do, acknowledge a George. Think about them, their moods, their cares, their excitements and pleasures, their queer costumes and strange ways, and the good tales they could have told. And when you go down into the bar, think of all the thrilling stories that have been told there.

And remember that, a hundred years from now, other travellers will probably be coming to that same inn, to the same room and the same bar, and they will order their drinks and think of the strange tales the inn could have told of the war that lasted six years' way back in the 1940's when atomic energy was just being developed. And they will think of you as a queer, old-fashioned thing, and wonder what strange tales you could have told of the inn as you knew it. And yours will be counted Tales of Old Inns then. For the English inn goes on.

# INDEX